THIS SOVEREIGN ISLE
Britain In and Out of Europe

Robert Tombs

ALLEN LANE
an imprint of
PENGUIN BOOKS

ALLEN LANE

UK | USA | Canada | Ireland | Australia
India | New Zealand | South Africa

Allen Lane is part of the Penguin Random House group of companies
whose addresses can be found at global.penguinrandomhouse.com

First published 2021

003

Set in 12.6/15.4pt Fournier MT Pro
Typeset by Jouve (UK), Milton Keynes
Printed and bound in Great Britain by Clays Ltd, Elcograf S.p.A.

The authorized representative in the EEA is Penguin Random House Ireland,
Morrison Chambers, 32 Nassau Street, Dublin D02 YH68

A CIP catalogue record for this book is available from the British Library

ISBN: 978–0–241–48038–0

Contents

Preface: Why This Book?   vii

1. Set in a Silver Sea   I
2. Joining 'Europe'   22
3. Second Thoughts   35
4. Divisions and Identities   60
   Who Voted and Why?   61
   Explaining 'Leave'   67
   Explaining 'Remain'   72
   Economic Worries and 'Project Fear'   78
   Narratives of Leave and Remain   85
   Culture Wars?   90
5. Stopping Brexit – Almost   97
6. COVID and After   126

Conclusion: 'Not in Our Stars'   150

Acknowledgements   163
Notes   165
Index   195

Preface: Why This Book?

'Our neighbours across the Channel, being made for
free trade by the maritime character of their economic
life, cannot possibly agree sincerely to shut themselves
up behind a continental tariff wall.'

Charles de Gaulle, 1970[1]

If anyone ever asks me what I did during the great lockdown,
the answer will be that I wrote this book. My intention had
been to start on a history of monotheism, but, as with many
others, my plans were altered by Brexit. I am old enough to
have voted in the 1975 referendum (to stay), and although
I was always suspicious of the ambitions and pretensions of
European federalists, the EU seemed a fact of life, like the
weather. After writing *The English and Their History* (to
which this book is in some ways an appendix), I was occasion-
ally asked to comment on and try to explain British political
developments, including for foreign readers. Before the 2016
referendum, I predicted in an American journal that David
Cameron would negotiate a compromise that would enable
the UK to remain a member of the EU. After some hesitation,
I voted Leave in 2016, and I recall two things that influenced
that decision. One was an open meeting in Cambridge at
which I asked the panel whether it might be better to stay in
the EU for the time being, and leave if or when its problems
became worse; and the reply by Dr Chris Bickerton (an expert
on EU affairs) was that the decision was now – there might

not be a second chance. The second, days before the vote, was dinner at a friend's house with the Nobel Prize-winning economist Kenneth Arrow, who had publicly opposed Brexit. I asked him whether leaving the EU meant economic disaster. He replied, 'No, there will need to be some adjustment, but certainly no disaster.' Had he said the opposite, I might have voted to Remain.

Although a piece I wrote in 2017 explaining Brexit to the readers of *Le Monde* elicited a rather splenetic letter of denunciation signed by seventy-four colleagues — something of a badge of honour — I was still more a commentator than an advocate. One reason this changed was the disdainful attitude of Remainers, both prominent and obscure: I remember a fellow guest at a party in Cambridge telling me that she had finally understood why people voted Leave because her gardener and cleaning lady had explained it. When it became clear that influential groups were trying to neutralize or overturn the referendum result, I was convinced that this was potentially disastrous. I cannot quite recall the circumstances that led a tiny group of academics, myself included, to set up a website towards the end of 2017 called Briefings for Brexit, but I do remember the motive: to ensure that economic analyses contesting the prevailing anti-Brexit orthodoxy could be made public. This was my first ever venture into politics. If it has perhaps cooled a few acquaintanceships, it has made many friendships.

This book is an offshoot of that activity. It is a history: not neutral, but I trust rational and I hope fair. I am a historian of France (and, by marriage, a citizen of the Republic), and have spent most of my career writing and teaching about European history. This book reflects that background. Though primarily concerned with the well-being and future of Britain, I am also concerned for Europe, with which I have many close ties; indeed, the future of Europe and its peoples now worries me more than that of Britain.

Why take a historical approach, rather than simply analysing the political forces and economic interests of the present day? Because our relationship with Europe, our internal divisions, the EU's evolution and its present travails can only fully be understood as the interplay of many different beliefs about the past. These beliefs create conflicting understandings of the present, diverging expectations of the future, and divided loyalties and identities. The past, if carefully interrogated, helps to explain what is happening; but no outcome is predetermined by history. The past shapes our ideas and has created the circumstances in which we find ourselves, but it does not dictate how the story continues. Those who claim that history is on their side are abusing it: and the abuse of history is one of mankind's oldest cultural endeavours.

I ended the final chapter of *The English and Their History* by quoting G. K. Chesterton — 'But we are the people of England; and we have not spoken yet' — and I added that 'No one had the faintest idea what they might say.' This book attempts to explain what they have now said, and why. By retracing the long history of these islands' relationships with their close Continent and the wider world, and then examining the more recent history of our illusions and disillusions concerning the 'European project', I am not suggesting that any choice was or is inevitable: indeed, I argue the opposite. The turbulence of the last few years has stemmed from the uncertainty of the outcome. Societies, like individuals, are doomed to choose their futures — an unforgiving but exhilarating fate.

1. Set in a Silver Sea

'Notwithstanding we are insulars, we are either by our
political or commercial interest connected with every
power in Europe.'

The Earl of Bute, secretary of state, 1762[1]

Geography comes before history. Islands cannot have the
same history as continental plains. The United Kingdom is a
European country, but not the same kind of European country
as Germany, Poland, or Hungary. The close Continent is the
mass towards which these islands gravitate, but which they
rarely join. For most of the 150 centuries during which they
have been inhabited, the mainland constituted their only connection. From across the narrow seas came opportunity and
danger, civilization and barbarism. Seen from the other direction, the islands were – when they registered at all – places
of mystery and oddity, on the edge, literally and culturally.

When they enter the record in the third century BC, it is
through Continental eyes, those of explorers and traders ven-
turing to the limits of the known world. Islanders no doubt
ventured to the mainland, but made no mark on its written history. The next thirteen centuries saw a succession of invasions
and conquests. The Romans, first under Julius Caesar, came,
went and returned in AD 43 to stay. Our earliest national myth
is Boadicea's bloody rebellion. Most of the archipelago was
forcibly attached for three centuries to what became Latin
Christian civilization, which left an indelible mark.

Yet that mark was almost effaced by peoples from the North, part of a great migration from beyond the empire – the 'barbarian invasions' – that shattered the Roman world and colonized its fragments. The islands were too remote to attract land invaders from the east, such as the Goths, Lombards and Franks, who eventually became the rulers of Iberia, Italy and Gaul. Instead, sea-borne raiders came. Warrior castes of 'Angles, Saxons and Jutes' (as Bede called them) transformed the culture of most of the islands, largely destroying or displacing Christianity, Latin, indigenous languages, and urban society and trade. For a time, they wrenched the islands towards the pagan cultures of the North. By the seventh century there were five main language groups, and the lowland areas were divided between several unstable kingdoms. Yet, remarkably, during the worst period of civilizational collapse and invasion, it was in the far reaches of the west and north of the islands that fragments of Christian culture survived and were cherished.

Here we see the primordial fact about the islands' history. Shakespeare's 'silver sea' is both highway and defence: mostly highway, sometimes defence. The sea is a natural barrier, by definition, but one that is easy to cross – unlike, for example, a great mountain range such as the Alps. Unless it is defended, the sea offers an open road. Hence, insularity had to be won the hard way,[2] and has only been secure during the last 250 years, sealed by Nelson at Trafalgar in 1805 – Hitler in 1940 quickly realized invasion was impossible. Until Nelson's time, the islands' history was one of innumerable raids and invasions, at least nine of which since the Norman Conquest have overthrown governments.[3]

The paganized, Germanized islands were eventually drawn

back into the orbit of Rome and Gaul. Re-Christianization began when the Roman monk Augustine arrived in Kent in 597. The kingdom of Northumbria became a renowned Christian cultural hub. Educational centres such as York, Jarrow and Lindisfarne provided teachers and missionaries: Bede of Jarrow and Alcuin of York had European reputations. King Offa of Mercia was on cordial terms with the Frankish Emperor Charlemagne, who had managed by the early ninth century to re-create a semblance of the Roman Empire in the west. The Anglo-Saxons, fighting back against incessant Viking invasions between 793 and 937, which destroyed most of their kingdoms, managed to consolidate power in the south, in the kingdom of the West Saxons – Wessex. Alfred 'the Great' (who became king in 871) and his son and grandson, Edward and Æthelstan, became the first rulers, indeed the creators, of the kingdom of the English.

'Englalond' became a wealthy and respected, though peripheral, part of the Latin world, and its king was recognized as the leading ruler of the islands in 'an informal maritime empire',[4] in which the northern and western parts remained divided into predatory and unstable polities. The empire of Charlemagne was partly a model for the English kingdom. However, the final great upheavals were about to take place, the last aftershocks of the centuries of 'barbarian invasions'. First, in 1016, Knut of Denmark (King Canute) conquered England, making it during his lifetime part of a North Sea empire with Denmark and Norway. After his death, independence was restored during the lifetime of Edward the Confessor until the most famous year in British history, 1066. Another Scandinavian invasion was crushed at Stamford Bridge in September, ending for good the long period when the islands were primarily in a northern orbit. Only nineteen days later, William 'the Conqueror' defeated the English army at Hastings, killed King Harold, assumed the English crown, and forcibly created a new and different European connection with the powerful and autonomous dukedom of Normandy, and hence with France.

Thus began a new epoch in the history of the islands which lasted four centuries. It had profound effects throughout England and beyond. A new warrior class – at first about 8,000 men – annihilated the Anglo-Saxon nobility and almost monopolized power and wealth. They were part of what has been called a Frankish 'aristocratic diaspora' from the now fragmented Carolingian empire, which seized new domains from England to Palestine.[5] By 1350, twelve of the fifteen monarchies of the Latin world were ruled by descendants of the Franks.

English language, literature, art and architecture were ruthlessly eliminated. English lost its position as Europe's richest written vernacular, though its writers used their skills to create the first written literature in French. Power and wealth were concentrated in fewer hands, and the dominance of the king increased. The Anglo-Saxon kingdom had been rich, powerful and efficiently governed, with limited external ambitions. Post-Conquest monarchs kept its institutions and developed a Common Law, so-called as it applied to all throughout the country. They extended their power into the turbulent lands later called Wales, Ireland and Scotland, even though Scotland, under a Normanized aristocracy, remained politically independent – as of course to a considerable extent it still is. They used England's wealth for their own purposes of European power politics. Several (the last being Henry VIII)

4

even fantasized about becoming Holy Roman Emperor, and made frequent promises (rarely fulfilled) to join Crusades against the Muslim powers in the Mediterranean; but from those epic struggles the faraway islanders generally kept clear.

On and off from 1170 to 1453, the French-speaking kings of England, who controlled first Normandy and later the huge duchy of Aquitaine, engaged in repeated struggles with the kings of France, up to half of whose nominal domains at times they controlled. The French, whenever they could, used the Scots, the Welsh and, later, the Irish against the English, and continued to do so as late as the 1790s. (Some might suspect they are trying again today.) In 1338 Edward III escalated the conflict by claiming the Crown of France – a claim maintained in practice until the 1540s, when Henry VIII made the last attempt to realize it, and symbolically until 1800. The English nearly succeeded after the victory of Agincourt in 1415, when Henry V of England was accepted as the heir to the throne of France. But they finally lost at the battle of Castillon in 1453. That disaster precipitated the 'Wars of the Roses' among the English royal dynasty and signalled a new epoch in European geopolitics. The idea of a unique relationship with France has surfaced repeatedly, whether as enemy or as ally. France is the only country since 1066 with which England or Britain has three times considered formal union: in the 1420s, in 1940, and in 1956.

During the four centuries following the Norman Conquest, England was a strong peripheral power, but never at the centre of European affairs politically or culturally. At different times, France, northern Italy and Germany were the focus of power and culture (as reflected, for example, in the French and Italian influences in the works of Chaucer and Shakespeare).

But not the British Isles. They, and particularly England, were suppliers of raw materials and purchasers of luxury goods. England was closely linked with the Low Countries and their wealthy textile industry, which used English wool. It was in Antwerp in 1338 that the claim to the French Crown was first proclaimed. The Low Countries' connection is another of the islands' long-term links with the Continent, and at times it became the most important – most crucially because it is from there that England can be most easily invaded. Protecting the Low Countries from a hostile takeover is something the islanders repeatedly fought for, most recently in 1793, 1914 and 1940.

Dramatic change came during the reigns of Henry VIII, Mary I and Elizabeth I, when England, and later Scotland and Wales, but – fatefully – not Ireland, underwent religious Reformation. The jurisdiction of the Papacy in England was explicitly rejected. The Act in Restraint of Appeals (1533) is often quoted: 'This realm of England is an empire' – that is, a fully independent sovereign. The Reformation led to more than a century of devastation across Europe, and split Latin Christendom permanently. The cultural and political divisions are still tangible across the Continent and in these islands too, where political loyalties still dimly (in Ireland not so dimly) shadow religious lines.

But the Reformation did not separate the islands from the Continent. For two centuries, it drew them more deeply in as allies or enemies of the great European Powers, the Habsburg Empire and France, and as defenders of the Protestant cause.[6] The cautious Elizabeth I gave financial or military support to Protestant rebels in Scotland, France and the Netherlands in the 1580s. The Spanish Armada failed in 1588 to transport an invading Spanish army from the Netherlands to England. Elizabeth was herself offered the crown of the newly independent Dutch provinces, which she prudently declined. When the Stuart king of Scotland, James VI, became king of England in 1603, a complex chapter of accidents began in which the islands descended into the bloodiest of the many civil wars in their history, which the eminent historian John Morrill has called 'the last of the European wars of religion'. An important element was disagreement about European policy: 'Puritans' wanted to join an anti-Catholic crusade. During a brief period of republican religious dictatorship, Oliver Cromwell failed to bring about a British-Dutch Protestant republic and then embarked on wars against both the Dutch and the Catholic Spanish. The restored Stuarts favoured Catholicism and closeness to the rising power of Louis XIV's France. The turbulence these policies caused ended in England and Wales – though not in Scotland or Ireland – when James II was deposed and the Three Crowns of England, Scotland and Ireland were jointly assumed in 1688 by the Calvinist ruler of the Netherlands, William of Orange, and his Protestant Stuart wife, Mary II.

This 'Glorious Revolution' was epoch-making politically, and it also introduced modern agricultural and financial methods from Holland. It did so at the cost of dragging the Three Kingdoms into an interminable series of wars against hegemonic France as an ally of the Dutch. The islands, thought a contemporary, had become 'the Cittadel . . . of Europe, where the Keys of her Libertys are deposited'.[7] After William's death in 1702, and then that of Queen Anne in 1714, the nearest Protestant heir to the throne, the electoral prince of Hanover, became King George I. This further added to Britain's

Continental commitments by linking it with a German state and giving it a stake in central European politics.

The deadly conflict with France – five of the eight bloodiest wars in world history[8] – has aptly been called 'the Second Hundred Years War', and it did not end until the victory of Waterloo in 1815. The consequences for Britain, Europe and indeed the world can hardly be overstated. The need for wartime unity led to political and religious compromise, the Bill of Rights (1689), the consolidation of the parliamentary system and the Union of England, Wales, Scotland (1707) and eventually Ireland (1800). The need for credit led to the emergence of the City of London as the world's main financial centre. The need for revenue to finance war led to the forceful pursuit of overseas markets and colonies. The new United Kingdom was rapidly transformed from 'European laughing stock to global great power',[9] and (roughly between 1750 and 1850) it became the first coal-powered industrial society.

Determining the proper international strategy for the United Kingdom aggravated the eighteenth-century political division between Whig and Tory. The Whigs, supporters of the 1688 Revolution and of the Protestant Succession of the Hanoverians, supported active involvement in European politics. The Tories, largely on grounds of cost, supported what was called a 'blue-water policy' of overseas trade and maritime power. Parallels with the present day have often been drawn.

Extra-European horizons opened for Britain, really for the first time. From the fifteenth century onward, Europe's chequered relations with the wider world had been pioneered by Portugal, Spain and Holland. England had lagged, merely acquiring Bombay and Tangier as part of Charles II's

Portuguese wife's dowry, grabbing a few Caribbean islands, and establishing agricultural settlements in North America, overshadowed by the French in Canada and Louisiana. Scotland had almost bankrupted itself by a colonial adventure in Central America in the 1690s – one of the reasons for embracing union with England. During the next century, Britain became a major participant in the 'triangular' Atlantic slave trade, supplying goods to African rulers in exchange for slaves, shipping the slaves to Spanish, French and Portuguese colonies and to their own, and then bringing back sugar and other tropical products to Europe. Spilling over from the struggles in Europe, a series of wars during the 1740s, 50s and 60s gradually made British power predominant in India and North America at the expense of the French, culminating in the Seven Years War (1756–63), which Churchill called the real first world war. The French got their revenge by helping thirteen of the American colonies to independence in the early 1780s, but Britain kept its quasi-monopoly of American trade. Thus was decided the future of the West and the world balance of power well into the twentieth century.

The islands attained a cultural prominence in Europe that they had never before enjoyed. In the 1720s, there began a lengthy vogue for their literature, fashions, ideas and institutions. Shakespeare (via French translation) became a name known across Europe, along with Isaac Newton, John Locke and, later, David Hume, Daniel Defoe and Adam Smith. For the first time, people began to learn the language, including even the king of France, Louis XVI. This reflected Britain's new wealth and military success, which culminated in the defeat of Napoleon. The Romantic period saw English and Scottish literature and art attain European status. The English language began to be used internationally. British political institutions were widely emulated: two-chamber parliaments, parliamentary control of the budget, ministerial responsibility, party organization, press freedom. British sports became the newest form of sociability, first for the upper classes and then the new urban masses on every continent.

These fundamental changes inevitably altered the United Kingdom's security strategy and its view of the world. For much of the Middle Ages, English and Scottish policy had revolved round English territorial possessions in France, with the Scots periodically members of an 'Auld Alliance' (1295) with the French. The Reformation changed the game: England and then Great Britain (as James VI and I called his kingdoms) felt that their security and basic liberties required them to resist the Continental hegemony of new Catholic powers, first the sprawling Habsburg Empire (Spain and Spanish America, much of Italy, much of Germany, and the Netherlands), and then Louis XIV's France. The new strategy was to aid those resisting these superpowers with money, ships and even troops, and to use diplomatic efforts to encourage coalitions against the hegemon.

Despite being among the smaller and weaker European states from the fifteenth to the eighteenth century, the British had advantages. Their island position gave a degree of protection as long as they could muster the naval strength to dominate the Channel and the North Sea – far from self-evident, as the French came uncomfortably close to invading England in 1715, 1745, 1779 and 1804, and were repeatedly able to land small forces in Scotland, Ireland and Wales. Britain's growing domestic economy and overseas trade, harnessed by a notably efficient taxation and credit system, gave it the money to fight, to subsidize less solvent allies, and eventually to build up its naval strength to a level of absolute superiority: 'the largest, longest, most complex and expensive project ever undertaken by the British state and society.'[10] This strategy culminated in the wars against Revolutionary and Napoleonic France. Britain took part in seven coalitions against France between 1793 and 1815, and by the end was subsidizing the war effort of all its allies, including Prussia, Austria, Russia, Spain and Portugal. This gave the United Kingdom the ability to influence the post-war development of Europe as one of its guaranteeing powers: its aim was to preserve European peace after 1815 by co-operation among the Great Powers, marking a new and more peaceful phase in the history of the Continent.

During the nineteenth century, Britain's involvement with the world beyond Europe accelerated. Its empire, in which the Scots and Irish were particularly active, continued to grow. Eventually (if briefly) it covered a quarter of the globe, made possible by the widespread fluidity and fragility of existing political systems. The islands' population boomed, largely because wider prosperity meant earlier marriage: despite mass emigration, it doubled between 1811 and 1891. More food had to be imported, as did raw materials for the new industries that sustained living standards. Sir Robert Peel, prime minister between 1841 and 1846, regarded this as inevitable: he thought one 'might on moral and social grounds prefer cornfields to cotton factories [but] our lot is cast, and we cannot recede'.[11] From the 1840s (under the pressure of a Europe-wide food shortage, devastating in Ireland) Britain adopted a policy of free trade, both as an economic necessity and as an idealistic mission to bring global peace and prosperity. The world entered the first age of globalization, centred on Britain's large domestic market, uniquely open to overseas exporters. A growing share of food and raw materials came from the United States, Argentina and the Empire. British exports shifted from the near Continent to the Americas, Asia and the Pacific. A large part of the world's railway system was built with British expertise, capital and equipment; trans-oceanic shipping was overwhelmingly British, as was the global telegraphic network; and the City of London became the global financial centre. France, Europe's other global power, though it attempted to maintain rivalry with Britain, was always in reality far more focused on Europe politically and economically, and it set up no major overseas settlements. Even Algeria, nominally part of France, was largely colonized by people from Italy and Spain.

Population growth across Europe meant unprecedented levels of emigration. Over the nineteenth century, some 10 million people left the British Isles, mainly for the United States, Canada, Australia, New Zealand and South Africa. For the first time, Britain had a significant overseas population in settler colonies which, while sometimes restive and determined on autonomy, regarded themselves as British. By around 1900, some 90 million people outside the islands spoke English as their native language. Visionaries such as the Birmingham radical Joseph Chamberlain hoped to create a global imperial federation. The United States of America, emerging economically and demographically as a great power of the future, was, it was hoped, a natural partner. Although relations with the Americans had long been touchy, including a war in 1812 and several subsequent crises, both sides shunned conflict.

Although the victory over Napoleon had given the United

Kingdom a leading role in Europe, it soon pulled out of attempts by the Russian-sponsored 'Holy Alliance' – perhaps the first modern attempt at supranationalism – to impose an authoritarian European order ('sublime mysticism and nonsense', thought the foreign secretary, Lord Castlereagh). Instead, Britain became the promoter, and sometimes the protector, of independent liberal states, including France, Belgium, Greece, Spain and Portugal. It also began its long, single-handed campaign against slavery, using persuasion, bribery, threats and (where necessary) force to change what had been a universally practised and legal institution into a criminal activity. This caused friction with many other countries, including France, the United States, Spain, the Ottoman Empire and slave-trading African kingdoms.

Britain was never a superpower, but always a medium-sized state 'attempting to maintain the largest Empire the world has ever seen with armaments and reserves that would be insufficient for a third-class Military Power'.[12] Inevitably, it had to prioritize, and so became steadily less involved in a Europe that decreasingly threatened its security or fulfilled its economic needs. But there was not a binary choice – perhaps there never has been or will be – between being 'in' or 'out' of Europe. As Castlereagh (perhaps our greatest foreign secretary) put it in his famous State Paper of 1820, Britain would act 'when actual danger menaces the System of Europe', but 'this Country cannot, and will not, act upon . . . abstract and speculative principles', especially if this meant interfering in the 'Self-Government' of other countries.[13]

Britain's ideal was a peaceful, free-trading Europe. A Commercial Treaty with France in 1860 initiated what has been called the first Common Market,[14] though it was eventually nullified by French and German protectionism, and experiments with a single currency were wrecked by Italian overspending. Although security fears remained, including rather absurd ones such as vetoing a Channel tunnel in 1883 for fear of French invasion, it was events in the Middle East, China, India, the Americas and Africa that now demanded most attention. Britain's only involvement in a major European conflict during this period – the Crimean War against Russia – was motivated by concern for the Middle East more than Europe. Britain made little effort to shape the unification of Italy during the 1850s, and watched with limited concern and negligible influence as the separate German states were turned by Otto von Bismarck into a new and powerful German Empire by aggressive wars against Denmark, Austria and France. Even had Britain wished to interfere it could scarcely have done so: it was perhaps 'a gendarme of the seas', but never 'a true global policeman'.[15] Bismarck joked that if the British landed their army in Germany, he would have it arrested, and Benjamin Disraeli declared that Britain 'was really more an Asiatic power than a European'. He was happy to encourage Bismarck to take the lead in maintaining Continental stability at the 1878 Congress of Berlin. Britain's main worries were France and Russia, but because of their imperial, not their European, ambitions. By the end of the nineteenth century, as one Canadian politician put it, Britain's global strategy was one of 'splendid isolation', a position it was very reluctant to abandon: its only military alliance was with Japan.

So when, for the first time since 1815, a general war broke out in Europe in July 1914, the response of the United Kingdom was uncertain: 'there seems no reason', thought Prime Minister H. H. Asquith, 'why we should be anything more than spectators.'[16] But when Germany invaded neutral Belgium and attacked France, most people accepted that ultimately Britain was a European state, that its security and vital interests depended on a stable and not unfriendly Continent, and that it must therefore combat the aggressors. The human and material costs were huge, including the breaking away of Ireland from the Union.

Supporters of British membership of the EU have invoked the world wars as a clinching argument, notably David Cameron in May 2016: 'Whenever we turn our back on Europe, sooner or later we come to regret it. We have always had to go back in, and always at much higher cost.'[17] Leading historians are not so sure. Some argue that Britain would have done itself and Europe more good by staying neutral in 1914, limiting the spread and duration of the conflict. Less blood would have been shed, Europe would have been less poisoned by hatred, and Britain itself left stronger.[18] A similar argument has been made, if less plausibly, for the Second World War.[19] Be that as it may, no one has convincingly shown how Britain could have prevented war in 1914 or 1939.

When peace finally came, Britain was one of the 'Big Four' in the 1919 peace negotiations in Paris. Many politicians, diplomats and commentators believed that the Allies were too harsh with Germany – a view popularized by the economist John Maynard Keynes. Almost from the beginning, an idealistic current appeared, strongest in progressive circles but shared in all parties: broadly, that the age of war must end, disarmament and reconciliation be embraced, and future relations between states be founded not on military alliances but on international solidarity via the new League of Nations. The vision of a United States of Europe embodying 'the

European soul' (sometimes tinged with anti-Americanism, anti-Semitism and impatience with workaday democracy) attracted foreign-policy theorists and utopians of every stripe from communist to fascist ('all Europe is my home', proclaimed Sir Oswald Mosley).[20] Economic initiatives – a Steel Cartel (1926), an Oslo Agreement (1930) and a series of Rome Protocols (1934) – were also pursued. At the same time came diplomatic attempts to appease Germany, both before and after the arrival in power of Adolf Hitler in 1933. In Britain, part of the aim was to limit involvement in European politics: Winston Churchill in 1933 wanted Britain to 'stand aside' from cross-Channel conflicts: 'I hope and trust that the French will look after their own safety, and that we shall be permitted to live our life in our island . . . we have to be strong enough to defend our neutrality.'[21] Nevertheless, Britain did not 'turn its back', but took on the leading role in trying to keep the peace. 'Appeasement' was in part a sincere determination to prevent another war, and in part a realization that the maintenance of imperial power and security, from Palestine to Hong Kong, and from Ulster to South Africa, could not easily be combined with a major Continental commitment.

Appeasement reached its nadir with the abandonment of democratic Czechoslovakia to Hitler in 1938–39. Thereafter, most people and politicians realized that a second war – not only with Germany, but with Italy and Japan too – was increasingly likely, and could only be sustained through a national effort to which all other interests would have to be sacrificed. It was still hoped that a strong deterrent air force and the world's most powerful navy could keep danger at bay – as long as France could bear the main burden of fighting on land. Hitler provoked war in September 1939. The

British and French were convinced that in a long war they would prevail. They should have been right, for in population, economic capacity, access to global resources and even in military force they were far stronger than Germany. But an audacious gamble by the German army in May 1940 tore up the balance sheet.

The defeat of France, completely out of the blue – even Hitler was astonished – transformed the strategic situation. Britain's European allies had fallen; Italy, Germany's main ally, had a powerful navy and air force in the Mediterranean; the Soviet Union was aiding Germany with oil and raw materials; collaborationist France and its empire were potentially hostile; America showed no sign of intervening; and Japan was a clear threat – it finally launched a simultaneous attack on the United States and the British Empire in December 1941. So, for a time Britain and the Empire were facing two, then three, major enemies spread right round the globe: a more formidable challenge than any empire in history has confronted. Churchill faced down pressure to seek peace and rallied the nation to fight – his unambiguous claim to the gratitude of humanity, for the alternative was to acquiesce in world domination by an alliance of genocidal fascist states.

Bombing, comprehensive conscription, mass labour mobilization and rationing brought the war home to every person more than ever before in modern times. Fortunately, Britain's enemies were not quite as strong as they looked, and the British economy was resilient. In a long war, with the peoples of the empire mobilized, and especially once America was drawn in, victory was certain. The oceans and the air were decisive. The Royal Navy continued to control the Western hemisphere, and hence access to global resources. The RAF, seconded by the American air force, devastated Germany's home front, forcing it to devote the lion's share of its war effort to air defence, stripping the Eastern Front and probably saving the Soviet Union.[22] But it was gruelling and expensive. It left Britain worn out and indebted, and the Empire was destined to unravel fairly quickly after 1945. The end of the war, with Europe in ruins, the Cold War between America and Russia pending, and the break-up of all the European empires accelerating, opened a new historical epoch, to which we shall turn in the next chapter.

Is there a pattern in this long and complex story of the relations between our offshore islands and the Continent? Does it dictate our proper present and future relationship with Europe, or even with the European Union, as many have suggested? It is tempting to say that the pattern is an absence of pattern. Our geography, with which I began, has favoured a range of different and temporary connections. It is barely even possible to say with which parts of Europe Britain has closest links and greatest affinities, politically or culturally. Once a province of Rome; invaded by north Germans and heir to a mainly Germanic language; briefly part of a Scandinavian empire; for four centuries in a violent relationship with France; for a time in a personal union with the Netherlands; and for more than a century through Hanover a power in Germany. It has been both the ally and the enemy of every great Continental state, Catholic and Protestant, monarchy, democracy and dictatorship. Its monarch even has a plausible claim to be a sherif of Islam, a descendant of the Prophet Mohammed.[23]

Two things seem clear, however. First, the islanders have never, since the 1550s, pursued or accepted a permanent organic Continental link. Earlier English kings claimed the French crown. Mary Queen of Scots hoped to unite Scotland, France and England. Mary Tudor, desperate to restore Catholicism, married Philip of Spain with the promise that their son would inherit a Continental empire combining England, the Low Countries and Burgundy. But the Reformation was a watershed. Even Scotland, despite its 'Auld Alliance', rebelled against French rule in 1559, aided by Elizabeth I. That same Elizabeth refused the crown of the Netherlands, just as she refused to marry a French or Spanish prince. Stuart plans for a Spanish marriage alliance were highly unpopular. William of Orange was never loved, and the Hanoverians and their territory in Germany were loathed as the source of expensive and dangerous European commitments. Britain rejected the 'Holy Alliance', and Victorian statesmen subsequently refused any permanent European tie. Once Britain entered into global enterprises in the eighteenth and nineteenth centuries, the Continent – though admired for its cultural glories and recreational charms – was widely considered a source of political difficulties, dangers and unwanted complications.

Second, Britain has never been tempted or forced to ally itself with the hegemonic Continental power of the day to share in the spoils of dominating Europe. It was the only major European state that never became an ally or a willing satellite of either Napoleon or Hitler. If national identity was important, twenty miles of sea were certainly no less so; and even more decisive was mastery of the oceans, enabling Britain to mobilize global resources to overcome Continental threats and work to create a 'balance of power'. Whatever the ambitions of certain politicians, the country has never made a serious attempt to join a triumvirate with France and Germany to control the European Union.

The islands have established over the last four centuries connections outside Europe that became in many ways closer and more attractive. The millions who emigrated in search of a better life did not cross the Channel or the North Sea but went to English-speaking countries outside Europe. Today, two and a half times as many British expatriates live in the 'Anglosphere' as in Europe, and Britain's main ethnic minorities are from Commonwealth countries.[24] This makes Britain more than a purely European nation. It is not the only one, of course. Portugal, Spain and France have extra-European connections, as to a lesser extent do Ireland, Holland, Italy and Belgium. But the differences are as clear as the similarities. Portuguese and Spanish colonies mostly broke away by force two centuries ago; and economic ties with South America do not approach the importance of those within the Anglosphere. In the case of France, imperial economic links were always far less important than for Britain. Although colonies provided military manpower for France during both world wars, this was incomparably less significant than the global Anglophone alliance. Moreover, the French empire ended in blood and hatred to a far greater extent than did the British. Most importantly, the crucial alliance between English-speaking countries during the Second World War, which for all, even the United States, was indispensable to victory, had no parallel; and of course this relationship continued during the Cold War and remains today, whatever the vagaries of passing politicians, the bedrock of British and Western security.

The rest of this book examines why, between the 1950s and 1970s, Britain changed its stance towards the Continent.

Instead of maintaining loose, oscillating relationships with its neighbours, it joined an embryonic federation. Then, after four decades, it changed its mind again, amid much recrimination. Now it looks as if the uneasy attempt to place the islands 'at the heart of Europe' has been merely one more geopolitical fantasy, like Plantagenet ambitions to be Holy Roman Emperors or kings of France.

2. Joining 'Europe'

'A democracy can abdicate in two ways, either by giving all powers to an internal dictator, or by delegating those powers to an external authority which . . . in the name of economic well-being will dictate monetary, budgetary and social policy, and finally policy in the broadest sense, both national and international.'

Pierre Mendès-France, former
French prime minister, 1957[1]

'The true purpose of the Community is security as well as prosperity . . . Its objectives, whatever the forms through which they first expressed and still express themselves, are not usually economic.'

Sir Con O'Neill, 1972[2]

The end of the Second World War saw Europe in a state of chaos and destruction unseen for centuries. The Continent's nation states were in ruins, materially, politically and, in some cases, morally. Of the twenty-six existing in 1938, by the end of 1940 ten had been occupied by hostile powers, four divided up, three annexed, and two reduced to satellite status. The leading Labour Party intellectual Harold Laski was one of many predicting during the war that 'the age of the nation state is over . . . economically, it is the continent that counts: America, Russia, later China and India, eventually Africa . . . the true lesson of this war is that we shall federate the Continent or suffocate.' For people of all countries and all parties, the idea of a united Europe was a breath of hope.

There was none of the 'war to end war' optimism of 1918: events had shown the hollowness of such ideals. Merciless Soviet takeovers in Eastern Europe seemed a possible prelude to further advances, abetted by communists in the West. No one could rule out that a defeated Germany, as after 1918, might seek revenge. The Americans might again retreat into isolation. So no British government could contemplate the semi-detachment from European politics that its predecessors had vainly pursued between the wars. On the contrary, Britain became an active pioneer of European organization.

The 1945 Labour government, and its forceful foreign secretary, the trade unionist Ernest Bevin, aimed to create a 'Western Union', centred on a Franco-British partnership, taking in the Benelux countries, Scandinavia and eventually a democratic Germany, creating links with British, French and Belgian African colonies and independent Commonwealth countries. This, Bevin believed, would make a unit economically and militarily strong enough (with a nuclear deterrent) to act as an equal with the United States, and resist the Soviet threat; and he hoped soon to have the Americans 'eating out of our hand'.[3] The first step was the Franco-British Treaty of Dunkirk (1947), followed by the Treaty of Brussels (1948) with the Benelux countries. 'Harmonization' in economic matters and common social and cultural policies were promised, and Bevin looked forward to a common market and a common currency. It has recently been argued that this Franco-British partnership might indeed have become the core of a united Europe.[4] However, it was stillborn, a victim of the onset of the Cold War and the consequent need for American protection.

Britain and France persuaded the United States to join a permanent security organization, and the North Atlantic Treaty was signed in April 1949, to last in the first instance for ten years. Bevin came to see Britain's role less as the European leader with France than as the 'pivot' or bridge between Europe and America.

London pushed consistently for intergovernmental organizations, such as the Organization for European Economic Cooperation, the Council of Europe, and the Western European Union. Support in Britain for supranational integration was very limited. Churchill's views wavered. He had spoken favourably of a 'United States of Europe' in 1946, but on the assumption that Britain would not be a member. Bevin thought the same: 'Great Britain was not part of Europe; she was not simply a Luxembourg.' Painful memories of the previous generation suggested that European partners were neither strong enough nor reliable enough to be the buttress of British security. As Bevin saw it:

> The people in this country were pinning their faith on a policy of defence built on a Commonwealth–USA basis – an English-speaking basis . . . How could he go down to his constituency – Woolwich – which had been bombed . . . and tell his constituents that the Germans would help them in a war against Russia?[5]

Trade and economic policy pointed to the same conclusion. Since the 1930s Depression, trade had moved outside Europe, especially to the Empire and Commonwealth, aided by sterling payments and preferential tariffs. In 1950, Europe, though reviving, took only 10 per cent of British exports, while the

Commonwealth and colonies took over 50 per cent. Labour's nationalization of the coal and steel industries meant that government and unions were unwilling to relinquish control to an unaccountable body in Luxembourg, the European Coal and Steel Community, set up in 1951 – the meaning of Deputy Prime Minister Herbert Morrison's famous comment that 'the Durham miners won't wear it'.[6]

Supranationalism was primarily backed by the USA and France. America sought a buttress against communism and a single organization it could deal with and which, moreover, would flatteringly mirror itself: it 'pursued unswervingly the goal of [a] United States of Europe as a heavenly city profiled on the horizon'.[7] One of the ' fathers of Europe', Jean Monnet, long resident in America, was influenced by these wishes.[8] For France – the first country to propose European confederation, back in the 1920s – the prime motive was to control Germany; and so it remains. In addition, France wanted a solid post-imperial foundation for continuing a global role, which leadership of Europe would provide. The Schuman Plan – influenced by Monnet and proposed with American encouragement in a speech by the French foreign minister Robert Schuman in May 1950 – provided for control of the coal and steel industries of Germany, France and the Benelux countries. Schuman was no European idealist, but saw France's interest: without coal and steel, no military threat; and, even more alluringly, 'an integrated area . . . which France would dominate.'[9] The plan advocated a council of ministers, a court and an assembly. The Treaty of Paris (April 1951) duly set up the European Coal and Steel Community, with an explicit commitment to political unity. West Germany, occupied by Allied troops, was willing to follow France's lead to rehabilitate itself as an international partner – this was 'our breakthrough', said Chancellor Konrad Adenauer, who, moreover, feared the 'Asiatic barbarism' of the USSR. The other original members, Italy and the Benelux, had their own reasons, which included having a share in collective decision-making. However, by the late 1950s, the Community seemed to be failing,[10] and there was speculation that Holland, Belgium and even France might seek to join the Commonwealth. An attempt to 'relaunch' integration produced the Treaty of Rome, signed in March 1957, setting up the following year a European Economic Community (EEC), committed to 'ever closer union'.

There was reason to assume that Britain would steer clear, as it did for several years. For those who later supported British membership of the EU, this delay was a terrible mistake, 'Britain's original sin'[11] from which all later problems flowed. The assumption is that Britain, with the prestige of victory, would naturally have assumed leadership and shaped integration to serve its interests. Precisely how this would have been done is rarely explained. Alan Milward, the official historian of Britain's European policy, states bluntly that the notion that Britain could have taken the helm 'is shot through with nationalistic assumptions . . . Europe was not asking to be led. It had not so many shared interests with Britain.'[12] Yet the idea that a great opportunity had been lost became a cast-iron myth, leading to the conclusion that Britain must never be left behind again, whatever the cost.

Why did Britain change policy? It happened suddenly under the Conservative government of Harold Macmillan. The reason was alarm, especially within the political and administrative establishment, that post-imperial Britain was being marginalized and was in other ways failing. 'If we try to remain aloof,' a Cabinet committee warned in 1960, 'bearing in mind that this will be happening simultaneously with the contraction of our overseas possessions, we shall run the risk of [losing] any real claim to be a world Power.'[13] It became an established assumption that the remedy was to move away from the Commonwealth and towards Europe.

Much of the alarm was economic. British industry was losing world market share: German car exports overtook those of Britain in 1955–56. The economy was growing more slowly than in Italy, Germany and France. Various explanations emerged, but most assumed deep-seated national failings: a culture that inhibited enterprise, inadequate technical education, lack of state planning, or non-membership of the EEC and partial exclusion from its dynamic market – in short, 'a culture of declinism that has persisted ever since'.[14]

No less urgent for Whitehall and Westminster was belief that Britain (and hence its governing elite) was losing status and influence. The fiasco of the 1956 Suez Crisis was 'a storm so sudden and violent as to threaten a complete change of course'.[15] As Sir Con O'Neill, the Foreign Office official subsequently in charge of negotiations to join the EEC, put it: 'What mattered was to get into the Community, and thereby restore our position at the centre of European affairs.'[16] Otherwise, 'our decline towards isolation and comparative insignificance, which it seems to me has already begun, is likely to continue, and cannot be arrested': Britain was in danger of becoming merely 'a greater Sweden'.[17]

These motives weighed heavily on several generations of policy makers and resurfaced during the Brexit debate: the need to be part of the club was paramount and the details of membership secondary. Given the historic importance of the policy thus initiated, the huge economic and political commitment it involved, and – not least – the turmoil and division caused in extricating the country sixty years later, it is astonishing how insubstantial, even illusory, their analyses have turned out to be.

First, Britain's relative economic failings and the Europeans' successes. These were based on comparative GDP growth statistics, first available in the 1950s. For pessimistically inclined observers they confirmed a declinist narrative of British economic history that went back to the slump of the 1920s or even to the later nineteenth century, when German manufacturing competition was first felt. An official report in 1954 warned of 'relegation of the UK to the second division'.[18] In reality, the British economy had performed extremely well during the war: better than those of Germany, Japan and Russia, and outpaced only by the USA.[19] By 1950, the British economy had narrowed the late-nineteenth-century productivity gap with America, and was far ahead of the Continent. It was in key areas the world leader, including nuclear power and aeronautics. But Continental economies were recovering from wartime devastation: Britain could hardly maintain its 50 per cent of world car exports once European industry returned to production. Germany's 'economic miracle' took place before 1952, and thereafter productivity growth was the same as Britain's.[20] Italy and France were still developing, redeploying large agricultural labour forces into industry and services. France, for example, had needed 1 agricultural worker to feed only 5.5 people in 1946, but by 1975 1 worker fed 26 people, and the rural workforce fell by nearly three-quarters.[21] So both countries enjoyed a generation of spectacular growth with dazzling signs of modernity – cars, music, films, fashion. Italy, the most economically backward of the three, for that reason enjoyed the highest growth of all over the period 1950–2000. Britain, on the other hand, was a mature industrial economy, with no peasant labour force to redeploy. To compare its performance (starting from a much higher level) with those benefitting from windfall growth was an elementary misunderstanding of economics, especially when it led to Britain being labelled 'the sick man of Europe'.[22]

A more appropriate comparison would have been with the United States: since 1944 (to the present day, in fact) British per capita GDP growth rates have kept in step with those of America.[23] So the most important public argument for applying to join the EEC, Britain's supposed economic failure, was illusory. Never was it clear precisely what economic benefits were supposed to be gained by joining. Never since has it been clear what benefits – if any – subsequently materialized. Looking back thirty years later, a major history of European integration concluded that: 'The United Kingdom has gained the least from membership . . . The economic case for British membership is probably the weakest of any member-state.'[24]

Economics, however, were not the decisive consideration for those making the decisions: for them, membership of the EEC was about power, to impress the United States and the Commonwealth with Britain's continuing importance. A former American secretary of state, Dean Acheson, greatly annoyed the British by putting publicly into words in 1962 what they hoped nobody else had noticed: 'Great Britain has lost an empire, and has not yet found a role.' From this viewpoint, the details of EEC economic policy and its future costs and benefits were secondary. 'None of its policies was essential to us; many of them were objectionable,' admitted O'Neill in private.[25] Similarly with the political and constitutional implications. The lord chancellor, Lord Kilmuir, pointed out that acceding to the Treaty of Rome 'would go far beyond the most extensive delegation of powers . . . that we have ever experienced'. Macmillan concluded that the aim was 'to live with the Common Market economically and turn its political effects into channels harmless to us'.[26] Public discussion of these fundamentals was, as far as possible, avoided, or, if unavoidable, their importance was minimized.

Let me try to summarize this post-imperial mindset. Britain had ruled the world's largest empire, which was melting away. The attempt to create a post-imperial Commonwealth as an obedient instrument of British policy had failed. Britain had, until about 1944, been a superpower equal to the Russians and the Americans, but now was not. It was therefore in danger of becoming insignificant – 'a greater Sweden' – but leadership of the EEC could give it new power and influence.

This was an understandable view of the world for that generation – and indeed it persists today[27] – but again it is clear with hindsight how weak were its foundations. First, having an empire had not been the source of Britain's power or wealth. After the adoption of free trade in the 1840s, the profits of empire, if 'not entirely negligible', were at most 5 or 6 per cent of national income by 1914.[28] Empire had been in many ways a political, strategic and economic liability, 'a brontosaurus with huge, vulnerable limbs which the central nervous system had little capacity to protect, direct or control.'[29] Britain's power had often been stretched to the limits, as Victorian statesmen were uncomfortably aware; and to consider it a sign of national decline that it could not muster the same forces as the United States was absurd. Compared with its old rivals France and Germany – and even, as it may now seem in retrospect, Russia – Britain has more than held its own, both militarily and economically. Finally, Whitehall hugely exaggerated the future power of the EEC: 'The Community may well emerge as a Power comparable in size and influence to the United States and the USSR,' whereas 'our diminished status would suggest only a minor role for us in international affairs.'[30]

A strange pessimism was at work here that insisted on comparing Britain only with the fastest-growing economies, and politically only with continent-sized superpowers. It shows a nostalgic obsession with boyhood memories of a Victorian golden age of unrivalled power which had never really existed, of all-conquering gunboats and imperious proconsuls in cocked hats. Perhaps too it shows the desperation of an elite that found itself the butt of mockery from its own people as bumblingly incompetent and decadent: these were the years of the Suez fiasco, the satire vogue, and a series of demeaning scandals involving treason, or sex, or both. Membership of the EEC was to cure the nation's imaginary malaise, regild the prestige of its elite, and find it a 'role'.

The cure, however, was not so easily obtained. Britain's first preference in the late 1950s was a free-trade agreement with the EEC, which would also allow trade with the Commonwealth and the wider world. This is what we had attempted in the 1860s, and it is hardly necessary to point out that it is where we appear to be heading back to in the 2020s. It would certainly have been more favourable to developing countries, unlike the protectionism and dumping of the Common Agricultural Policy, 'postwar Europe's most disgraceful economic policy'.[31] The Germans favoured a free-trade agreement, but the French – General de Gaulle now again in power – vetoed it in November 1958: Europe as a mere free-trade area is anathema to the French, as it limits their ambition of creating a great European power. So Britain set up a European Free Trade Association (EFTA) in 1960, with Sweden, Denmark, Norway, Switzerland, Austria and Portugal, and later Finland and Iceland.

However, Washington disliked this as a distraction from its aim of an integrated Europe – and 'not upsetting the United States' was a decisive consideration for Macmillan. The Americans put pressure on London to accede to the Treaty of Rome and the government duly applied in July 1961. 'It is only full membership, with the possibility of controlling and dominating Europe,' wrote an optimistic official, 'that is really attractive.'[32] Commonwealth trade fell sharply as businesses and governments prepared for British concessions to the EEC: 'They're bound to join, whatever we say,' thought the prime minister of Jamaica.[33] It was only in the late 1970s, none the less, that Commonwealth trade was overtaken by that with 'the Six'.[34] Whitehall still assumed that it could make the EEC accommodate its non-European political and economic links, at least during a long transitional period. As Alan Milward put it, there was a general agreement in Britain to accept something that was not on offer.[35]

This became painfully clear in January 1963 when General de Gaulle publicly vetoed Britain's application on the grounds that it was not sufficiently European: 'England [*sic*] is an island, sea-going, bound up, by its trade, its markets, its food supplies, with the most varied and often the most distant countries.' As he said privately to his aides, 'I want her naked.'[36] Despite the Labour Party's suspicion of the EEC, the next prime minister, Harold Wilson, renewed Britain's application in 1966, without preconditions. Like their predecessors and successors, Wilson and his colleagues persuaded themselves that once inside the club they would steer Europe in a British direction: 'if we can't dominate that lot,' said Wilson, 'there's not much to be said for us.'[37] After de Gaulle's retirement in the wake of the student riots of May 1968, his successor, Georges Pompidou, gave way: as he admitted to his entourage, only de Gaulle had the prestige to veto Britain's entry. Edward Heath's Conservative government seized the opportunity with alacrity. They accepted a Common Fisheries Policy, which made national fishing waters a common resource – a 'bolt from the blue' hastily agreed by the existing members on the day negotiations started.[38] (Norway baulked at this condition and stayed out.) Another portentous change was Pompidou's insistence in 1969 that the EEC should commit itself to 'economic and monetary union', which he hoped would be the means of containing Germany.[39] Sir Con O'Neill thought that there was only one possible response to the EEC's demands: 'Swallow the lot, and swallow it now.'[40]

Belief that membership was necessary at any price had become the orthodoxy in official circles: 'the terms were irrelevant', because Britain was 'the sinking Titanic', and Europe the 'lifeboat'.[41] The government mounted the biggest publicity campaign since the war, with vociferous support from business and most of the intelligentsia. The issue was carefully depoliticized: 'The Community . . . hasn't made the French eat German food or the Dutch drink Italian beer.' The EEC's faster economic growth was the selling point, represented on the front of an official pamphlet, *The British European*, by a model in a skimpy Union Jack bikini proclaiming: 'EUROPE IS FUN! More Work But More Play Too!'[42]

On 1 January 1973 Britain (with Ireland and Denmark) formally entered the EEC, celebrating with a 'Fanfare for Europe', including pop and classical concerts and poetry readings. But just as Britain finally clambered on board, the lifeboat sprang a leak.

3. Second Thoughts

'Let us not be afraid to say it: all the major decisions to move towards European integration . . . were the pure product of a modern form of enlightened despotism.'
                    Hubert Védrine, French foreign minister, 2002[1]

'We should never repeat our mistakes which led to our self-exclusion from the process which led to the signature of the Treaty of Rome . . . we would not want to find ourselves anywhere but in the central group.'
                    Crispin Tickell, FCO official, 1984[2]

In October 1973, nine months after Britain joined the EEC, war broke out between Egypt and Israel, leading to cuts in the supply of Middle Eastern oil and huge increases in the price. This caused economic havoc across the industrialized world and ended the halcyon period of post-war European growth. Ironically, the previously slow-growing Commonwealth economies have expanded faster than Europe's over the whole period since 1973.[3] So Britain's accession to a depressed EEC did not provide the hoped-for stimulus, and the country experienced two full years of recession. The Common Agricultural Policy (which supported farmers by keeping prices above world levels) increased British food costs, and the new Value Added Tax further raised consumer prices. Far from being lifted by membership of a dynamic trading bloc, the EEC system produced 'the maximum adverse impact on every single citizen of the United Kingdom'.[4] The outcome was 'stagflation', the debilitating combination of economic stagnation, rising inflation and rising unemployment. Thus began the economic and political turmoil of the 1970s, when Britain really did for a time seem to be the sick man of Europe. It had only four full years of economic contraction from 1945 to 2008, all of them between 1974 and 1981.[5] It was only between 1973 and 1979 that British manufacturing fell sharply behind that of the Germans.[6]

Opposition to British membership was strongest within the Labour Party and was shared both by left-wingers, for whom the EEC was a capitalist club, and by traditional Labour patriots worried about letting down the Commonwealth and compromising democratic institutions. The left-wing economist Nicholas Kaldor warned that the aim of 'economic and monetary union' would cause political and economic damage. Largely for party reasons, the Labour prime minister Harold Wilson stoutly declared in 1974 that he would 're-negotiate and de-negotiate' Edward Heath's accession terms and put the result to a referendum. The renegotiation – supposed to resolve, among other things, the Common Agricultural Policy, Britain's disproportionate budget contribution, and Commonwealth access to Europe's market – had no significant outcome, but it was represented as 'a New Deal in Europe'. Wilson, originally sceptical of membership, now mused that Britain was like 'a fading beauty' and the EEC a 'go-ahead young man with very good prospects'.[7]

On 5 June 1975 the referendum asked: 'Do you think that the United Kingdom should stay in the European Community (the Common Market)?' A former president of the European Commission 'deplore[d] a situation in which the policy of [the UK] should be left to housewives. It should be decided by trained and informed people.'[8] The Yes campaign was supported by 'all the acceptable faces of British public life', including Anglican bishops and most of the press. All echoed 'the golden thread of deceptive reassurance': it would make Britain more prosperous, but would change nothing that people cared about.[9] The campaign compared the Community with the United Nations and NATO, skirting round the fact that, unlike any other treaty organization, its rules were not fixed and it could legislate independently of Parliament. Those who voted Yes were most concerned about the economy, security and Britain's future place in the world; the Noes – urged on by the exotic and unpopular alliance of Enoch Powell, Tony Benn and the Ulster loyalist leader the Revd Ian Paisley – about food prices, national sovereignty and the Commonwealth.[10] Least keen on Europe were Scots, Ulstermen and the Left – the mirror image of 2016. The English, especially Tory voters from the prosperous south, were keenest: 64.6 per cent of the English electorate voted (well below the 2016 figure); of those, 68.7 per cent voted Yes. The left-wing historian E. P. Thompson commented that 'arrangements convenient to West European capitalism blur into a haze of remembered vacations, beaches, bougainvillea . . . and vintage wines.'[11] Margaret Thatcher, the new leader of the Opposition, hailed 'this excellent result'.

The economic and social turmoil of the 1970s were to transform Europe and the EEC. It began to undermine the communist system in Eastern Europe. And it brought Margaret Thatcher to power in the UK (in 1979), and the socialist François Mitterrand in France (in 1981). They adopted diametrically opposing policies for dealing with economic failure and were to transform a comatose EEC by simultaneously pursuing conflicting aims. Thatcher believed that her tough neo-liberalism would succeed in Britain and could equally galvanize Europe. Mitterrand's 'socialism in one country' failed disastrously, and his finance minister, Jacques Delors, was forced to abandon it. But Mitterrand and Delors concluded that, though France was too small for their policies to work, the EEC was big enough. Mitterrand began to press again for economic and monetary union (EMU). Its first stage, a 'European Monetary System' (EMS), was agreed in 1983 to co-ordinate the member states' exchange rates.

In 1984, the Thatcher government produced a plan to create a 'single market' in the EEC by removing major non-tariff barriers to internal trade. To overcome protectionist vested interests, the ability of individual states to block change was weakened by adopting 'qualified majority voting'.* This was institutionalized in the Single European Act (SEA) (1986), which has been described, somewhat tongue in cheek, as 'perhaps the greatest single contribution ever made to the construction of Europe', making Margaret Thatcher the 'founding mother of the new Europe'.[12] The European Commission and the German government acquiesced without noticeable enthusiasm. Later, Thatcher considered the SEA a terrible mistake, strengthening the EEC's federalizing and centralizing tendencies. But, at the time, she thought that it would move Europe closer to the traditional British aim of a free-trade area, with its political superstructure becoming redundant: 'A Community of sovereign states committed to

---

* By which European Council decisions are carried if 55 per cent of member states, representing 65 per cent of the EU population, support them.

voluntary co-operation, a lightly regulated free market and international free trade does not need a Commission in its present form.'[13]

This was a challenge to the French, who, since de Gaulle, had rejected a free-trade Europe. Mitterrand and Delors (who had become president of the Commission in 1985) were no exceptions. Delors set out to counteract the neo-liberal trend with new powers for the Commission to regulate the market and entrench social and economic protection. Rather than embracing Thatcherism, the EU would become a haven against it.

Delors ('one of the cleverest people I met in European politics,' thought Thatcher[14]) and his Commission adopted what they called a 'Russian doll' strategy, packaging integrationist measures together to make them easy to support and difficult to oppose. Thatcher called this a 'combination of high-flown rhetoric and pork-barrel politics',[15] and Brussels indeed became a huge centre for lobbying. There also began a programme of what Delors termed 'cultural management' – semi-official organizations, subsidized think-tanks, cultural activities, youth visits, prizes, endowed professorships, teaching projects, edifying schoolbooks, films and videos – to inculcate pride in being European and an acceptance that 'ever closer union' was the goal of history. 'We have made Europe, now we have to make Europeans,' wrote a leading French politician in a report for the Commission on 'the Europe of tomorrow'.[16] His readers would recognize that he was paraphrasing the nineteenth-century Italian nationalist Massimo d'Azeglio. Making peoples has proved a challenging task in both cases.

'Europe' thus became far more important in people's lives. The EU treaties acted as a supranational constitution, with supremacy over the legislatures of member states. European legislation acted directly on their courts. Fundamental decisions were made not by open debate and democratic voting, but by secret diplomatic bargaining behind closed doors. This 'counter-revolution' brought 'secrecy into the heart of domestic politics'.[17] What was called the 'democratic deficit'[18] became more obvious and more controversial – in the British case, with such minor but earthy examples as making it illegal to sell fruit and veg in pounds and ounces. As Delors admitted, 'European integration [was] practically contradictory [to] greater EC democracy.'[19] 'The people weren't ready to agree,' commented his senior aide, 'you had to get on without telling them too much.'[20]

The Thatcher–Delors clash came to a head in September 1988. Delors had recently told the European Parliament that within ten years he expected 80 per cent of economic legislation to be made in Brussels. Thatcher publicly criticized 'these airy-fairy ideas'. Delors addressed the TUC conference in Bournemouth on 8 September, knowing that Thatcher was to give a lecture to the College of Europe in Bruges a few days later. He won a standing ovation (with delegates singing 'Frère Jacques') by urging that 'social rights' should be guaranteed at European level. Thatcher regarded this as a deliberate provocation.

Her outspoken speech in Bruges – which dismayed the Foreign Office – criticized the direction the EU was taking. Although she stated that Britain was an essentially European country whose 'destiny' was as 'part of the Community' (though 'we have looked also to wider horizons'), she emphasized that the EU was not synonymous with Europe, that it was not 'an end in itself' and that 'it should not be a centralized

conglomerate', but be based on 'willing cooperation of sovereign states'. The most noticed phrase was taken as a direct
rebuttal of Delors' plans: 'We have not successfully rolled
back the frontiers of the state in Britain, only to see them
re-imposed at a European level with a European super-state
exercising a new dominance.'[21]

These rhetorical jousts had fundamental effects on British politics. For the first time since the early 1970s there was
open debate about membership and the future of the Community. Delors shifted Labour towards a pro-EEC position:
the party began to rely on Brussels to deliver policies that the
ballot box might reject. Thatcher's speech began the opposite
process for the Tories, dividing the party and alarming her
senior colleagues, none of whom endorsed her speech. For
Foreign Secretary Sir Geoffrey Howe it felt 'like being married to a clergyman who had suddenly proclaimed his disbelief
in God'. The European credo, he thought, 'does, has and will
require the sacrifice of political independence and the rights of
national parliaments. That is inherent in the treaties.'[22]

The following year came one of the greatest geopolitical
upheavals in modern European history: the rapid break-up
of the Soviet Union and the end of Communist Party rule
in Eastern Europe. An immediate issue for the EEC was the
future of Germany. All (including many Germans) regarded
the prospect of rapid German reunification with trepidation.
Thatcher and Mitterrand were both worried: he warned her
that 'they might make even more ground than Hitler'.[23] Both
began by trying to delay the process. But Mitterrand was
quicker on his feet: sensing the momentum, he shifted to getting the best deal for France, which, as ever, meant controlling
Germany. He vehemently demanded that Helmut Kohl, the

German chancellor, should commit rapidly to a 'European Monetary System' as a step towards 'political union'. That was the price of French support for reunification. The pressure was blunt: Germany had to prove it was 'a good European' or 'we will return to the world of 1913'. Kohl agreed in December 1989, saying 'Germany needs friends',[24] but he realized too that Germany had much to gain economically. The unspoken premise of this Franco-German relationship, thought the historian Tony Judt, was 'you pretend not to be powerful and we'll pretend not to notice that you are.'[25]

The French plan – it was overwhelmingly theirs – dated back to the 1950s: one can only admire the persistence of 'easily the most formidable, the best educated and most determined political class in Europe'.[26] Like most big European endeavours, it was politics under a skin of economics. A Delors Plan (April 1989) laid out three stages: one, an Exchange Rate Mechanism; two, a European Central Bank; and three, a single European currency, to be called the 'Euro'. This has been the most disastrous policy in the history of European integration: the Nobel Prize-winning economist Joseph Stiglitz calls it Europe's 'underlying mistake'.[27] Various monetary alignment systems had repeatedly failed over the decades, and yet the project was pushed forward regardless until the Euro was formally adopted in 1999. The single currency, as predicted, has periodically wrought havoc in the EU and has permanently damaged its weaker members, and, at the time of writing, the viability of the Eurozone is again in doubt.

There were arguments for the Euro that seemed plausible. Monetary 'stability', beginning with fixed exchange rates and culminating in the European currency, was presented as a means to efficiency (no exchange rate costs and frictions), and hence to rising productivity and employment, to 'convergence' between countries, and thence, via monetary and economic integration, to the nirvana of political union. This appealed to politicians and much of the public. But hardly any independent economists agreed that it was practically (as opposed to ideologically) desirable: the efficiency savings were negligible, but the dangers of inflexible currencies were stark among economies whose levels of performance were very different. British proposals for a more gradual policy were brushed aside.

Thatcher was reluctant to accept stage one of the Delors Plan but she found herself under great pressure to do so, most importantly from the chancellor, Nigel Lawson, and the foreign secretary, Geoffrey Howe. They gave her an ultimatum: either she would agree at the Madrid Council in June 1989 that the UK would take part in the Exchange Rate Mechanism, or they would both resign. Delors said later that this was the moment at which 'the single currency might have remained a dead letter for years'.[28] Thatcher gave in. Later she demoted Howe, and Lawson resigned. This was the beginning of the end for Thatcher, and the start of a three-decade-long feud within the Conservative Party in which most of the 'grandees' remained pro-integration, while the rank and file became increasingly Eurosceptical.

Another public clash with Delors started the endgame. He had again advocated a shift of power to European institutions. In the House of Commons on 30 October 1990, Thatcher responded that 'Mr Delors said . . . that he wanted the European Parliament to be the democratic body of the Community, he wanted the Commission to be the Executive and he wanted the Council of Ministers to be the Senate. No. No. No.'[29] The leader of the Labour Party, Neil Kinnock, retorted that 'her tantrum tactics will not stop the process of change . . . All they do is strand Britain in a European second division.' Geoffrey Howe resigned from the government and made a quietly devastating speech on 13 November attacking Thatcher's position on Europe. His argument repeated the rhetoric of the previous twenty years: it was

> essential . . . not to cut ourselves off from the realities of power; not to retreat into a ghetto of sentimentality about our past . . . People throughout Europe see our Prime Minister's finger-wagging and hear her passionate, No, No, No . . . maximising our chances of being once again shut out . . . We dare not let that happen again.[30]

Nine days later, Thatcher was forced to resign, essentially defeated by the Europhile element in her party.

Her successor, John Major, was an orthodox pro-European, who declared it his aim to place Britain 'at the heart of Europe'. The Maastricht Council (December 1991) drafted a new treaty based on the earlier agreement between France and Germany to move towards a single currency. To induce the thrifty German electorate to accept the loss of their own solid deutschmark, it was agreed to forbid bailouts of weak countries, to establish a fully autonomous European Central Bank, and to impose a 'Stability and Growth Pact' limiting national budget deficits to 3 per cent. Chancellor of the Exchequer Norman Lamont pointed to the evident dangers: the former French president Valéry Giscard d'Estaing replied, 'The points you make are good, but it's going to happen.'[31] Lamont's warnings were echoed by a chorus of economists.

Major negotiated 'opt-outs' from the Euro and the Social Chapter of the Treaty, leaving Britain in what pro-Europeans called the 'slow lane' and further reducing its demonstrably limited ability to influence European financial policy. The Maastricht Treaty (February 1992) formalized the agreements of the Maastricht Council, and inaugurated a new European Union.[32]

In other ways the Major government wished to demonstrate its commitment to Europe. In 1991 Britain and France eagerly took the lead in a European initiative to end conflict in the collapsing Yugoslavia and prove their capacity to be the military leaders and guardians of Europe. The crisis was proclaimed 'the Hour of Europe', without American involvement. 'Defence in Europe is not an opt-out subject for us – like the Social Chapter,' declared Douglas Hurd, the foreign secretary.[33] However, Europe was not willing to make sufficient effort to stop the fighting, and by late 1994 Britain's Balkan policy was 'falling to bits around us'.[34] Eventually, after harrowing bloodshed, the Americans were brought in to sort it out.

Less tragic but no less humiliating was the outcome of the Exchange Rate Mechanism, fixing the values of the national currencies as a precursor to the Euro – a step supported by all British political parties and by business lobbies, and which at the rate the UK joined duly caused an economic recession. Three countries, France, Denmark and Ireland, were holding referendums to ratify the Maastricht Treaty. The prospect of the treaty being defeated encouraged massive, practically risk-free and highly profitable speculative attacks on ERM members, bringing currency devaluations in Finland, Sweden, Italy, Spain and finally Britain, forced chaotically out of the system on 'Black Wednesday' (16 September 1992). Four days later the French referendum gave the narrowest of Yes votes following a 'sort of revolt of the little people'.[35] Denmark voted No to the treaty, but was pressured to vote again the following year, producing a narrow Yes and triggering riots during which eleven people were shot by police in Copenhagen.[36] Although falling out of the ERM actually boosted Britain's economy, the Conservative Party's trump card – its reputation for relative economic competence – was shattered, paving the way for electoral defeat in 1997. Britain was left very chary of further monetary experiments.

The coming of the Euro, scheduled for 1999, was the outcome of a long and consistent ambition for 'economic and monetary union'. As many warned, it was destined for trouble: it 'defied economics, politics and history'.[37] Recklessly, countries that were economically and financially weak, notably Italy and Greece, were allowed and encouraged to join – including by the German chancellors Kohl and Gerhard Schröder. How could such a project be contemplated, when economists and bankers warned over and over again of the perils? Apart from ancestral French fear of Germany, it was an egregious example of the magical thinking that had dominated European integration since the beginning: that European unity was the tide of history; that all enlightened people supported it; and that political will would bring it about. The 'European train' was constantly about to leave the station; the only question was how quickly to jump on board. The dangers were compounded by capricious decision-making. Heads of state and government – whose mental processes are sometimes even now unfathomable – made fundamental decisions without public scrutiny, and almost always without deigning to consult or listen to public preferences.[38] As Jean-Claude Juncker, later president of the Commission, explained frankly, 'We decree something . . . If no clamour occurs . . . because most people do not grasp what had been decided, we continue, step by step, until the point of no return is reached.'[39]

The way to mitigate the dangers of a single currency covering countries with very different levels of productivity was textbook economics: the stronger members would have to support the weaker, where necessary by massive public spending and subsidy, just as wealthy regions of a single country support poorer regions. But bailouts and budget deficits had been formally ruled out from the beginning, and 'regional funds', though good publicity, were insufficient. Consequently, the gap between rich and poor countries would increase. The latter, unable to improve their competitiveness by devaluing their currencies, would be forced to reduce their costs by lowering living standards and increasing unemployment. This had been known since the days of the Gold Standard but seemed unacceptable in modern democracies. Yet it has happened in the EU.

The Labour government of Tony Blair, elected in 1997, had to decide whether to join the Euro. Business bodies such as the British Chambers of Commerce and the Confederation of British Industry were uncritically enthusiastic, the latter urging its members not to be swayed by 'ill-informed scare stories'.[40] Blair, of conventionally pro-European sympathies, was in favour (or at least wished to appear so), but he knew that 'giving up the pound' was unpopular, and feared losing the referendum that pressure from Sir James Goldsmith's Referendum Party had induced him to promise – a reasonable fear, as the only two countries to hold votes on joining, Denmark and

Sweden, have both voted No. The chancellor, Gordon Brown (Blair's bitter rival), and the Treasury realized how risky the Euro project was, and drew up 'five economic tests' to be fulfilled before Britain would join. As these were unlikely to be met, it postponed a politically tricky decision indefinitely. An influential Treasury minister, Ed Balls, wrote later that 'the decision not to join the single currency has been the most successful economic decision of the last thirty years.'[41] This is, if anything, an understatement. It saved Britain (and hence the global financial system) from probable disaster when the banking crisis hit in 2007, and again permitted fast financial action in the pandemic of 2020. Moreover, it meant that leaving the EU remained possible – and in the long run probable.

The post-1989 liberation of Eastern Europe led to the expansion of the EU to the east, though with misgivings on both sides. An Irish referendum voted against expansion in 2001, but this was dismissed: 'a referendum in one country cannot block the . . . project',[42] which went ahead without a treaty. The Irish reversed their vote. Expansion was generally supported by Britain, for whose rulers the European project had always been primarily about geopolitics; some thought it had the further advantage of making 'ever closer union' less feasible. As a sign of commitment, the Blair government allowed the immediate free movement of people from the new Eastern European member states – something that both France and Germany refused. Blair favoured immigration, telling the Confederation of British Industry in April 2004 that, 'There are half a million vacancies in our job market and our strong and growing economy needs migration to fill these vacancies.' Officials predicted 5,000–13,000 workers to come per year from Eastern Europe: over 600,000 came in five years, and by 2012 there were some 700,000 Poles alone resident in the UK.[43]

This was proclaimed wholly beneficial. But it evidently benefited some more than others: employers more than workers; the middle classes more than the working classes. Between 2005 and 2007, 540,000 incomers found jobs, and 270,000 British workers lost them.[44] For many people, this was the most tangible consequence of EU membership, and larger numbers started voting for the United Kingdom Independence Party (UKIP), founded in 1993 and led pugnaciously by Nigel Farage, which began to emphasize uncontrolled immigration from the EU. The party came third in the 2004 European Parliament elections, and second in 2009, without being represented at Westminster. But its rise put increasing pressure on the mainstream parties, and especially the Conservatives, and helped to make some sort of popular vote on the EU likely.

The expansion of the EU made its governance more complex. So, it was decided to push on to further integration. In 2002 a Convention met in Brussels to draw up an EU Constitution. This was to be put to referendums in several countries in 2005, including Britain. In both France and the Netherlands, governments made intense propaganda efforts to get the Constitution accepted. The Dutch tried to scare voters with threats of power cuts and television footage of Auschwitz and Srebrenica. The French declared that 'Napoleon would have voted Yes'. But both nations voted No – a result the former Labour leader and European Commissioner Neil Kinnock described as 'a triumph of ignorance'.[45] It was not wholly a surprise: France had nearly voted against the

Maastricht Treaty in 1992, and now public-sector workers and young people had shifted to No, fearing a threat to their jobs and conditions. Blair was able to cancel the British referendum, with opinion polls showing a huge majority against, on the pretext that the Constitution was defunct – 'I was off the hook'.[46] The country was not, however. In the opinion of one scholar, from this point on 'it is quite possible that Britain's membership could be sustained only so long as British governments could avoid holding any EU referendum. A No vote would have been likely whatever the question on the ballot paper.'[47]

The Dutch and French No votes at first seemed a body blow to the European project. Jean-Claude Juncker (prime minister of Luxembourg) 'tearfully suggested that Europe's voters be asked to vote again "until they get it right".'[48] Instead, the essentials of the constitution were simply adopted by international treaty – the Lisbon Treaty of 2007. 'The substance of the constitution is preserved,' the German chancellor Angela Merkel told the European Parliament: 'That is a fact.'[49] The Irish gave another No vote, against ratification of the treaty, and again were induced to reverse it.

As many economists had warned, the introduction of the Euro in 1999 brought negligible benefits, major disadvantages and huge dangers. Far from accelerating trade between Eurozone members, one of its main objects, that trade stagnated in the early 2000s, and in most countries economic growth actually declined after they joined the Eurozone.[50] There was a worse problem. When several member states in southern Europe changed their own currencies for the Euro, they did so at what turned out to be too high a conversion rate. Others, most importantly Germany and the Netherlands, did so at too low a rate. The system was supposed to bring about convergence, but it actually increased divergence. Southern Europe, whose costs became uncompetitively high, built up growing structural trade deficits with northern Europe. Normally, this would cause revaluations of the various currencies, but of course these no longer existed. Instead, the weak countries borrowed, and the strong countries lent, in the belief that somehow the EU made it all safe.[51]

The big beneficiary of the Euro has been Germany, because the undervalued Euro has boosted German exports. A recent German study calculates that in consequence Germans have gained on average 23,000 euros per head, and nearly all other countries have lost substantially, the Italians to the tune of 74,000 euros per head.[52] Germany has built up a huge export surplus – the largest in the world – which destabilizes other European countries and, indeed, the whole global system. This is still increasing: in 2019, Germany had the world's largest current account surplus ($276 billion) for the fourth consecutive year.[53] As the Eurozone is organized, there is no clear way out – except, fancifully, if Germany leaves it.[54] Many people believe that this is cynical German policy. I think the reality is less sinister, but more intractable. On one hand, most Germans are 'good Europeans' who want 'Europe' to succeed, as it absolves them from their terrible recent history. But for that very reason, they do not want to be its hegemonic power, and cannot imagine themselves as such. They do not therefore see why they should make financial sacrifices to support the system – indeed they convince themselves they are already paying too much. Moreover, German economic theory, which informs its European policy, is fundamentally different and more conservative than that of Britain, France and the USA.[55]

Thus the EU is burdened with a dominant member state that will not recognize its own power or accept the duty to others it entails.

Where Britain was concerned, the Euro increasingly distanced it from Europe. In the early decades of its membership of the EEC, more than half its exports went to the Continent. This share steadily diminished as the Eurozone underwent a series of crises and as markets outside Europe grew. The Single Market (which applies mostly to agricultural and manufactured goods, but not to services, where Britain has an advantage) gave little benefit. British goods exports to the EU grew extremely slowly after 1999, and barely at all after 2007, whereas exports to non-EU markets grew many times faster. By 2020 key UK industries such as machinery and cars sent over 60 per cent of their exports outside the EU.[56] Since the mid-1990s, UK economic growth has been higher than that of the Eurozone, yet it has a permanent structural trade deficit, as the Single Market and Customs Union cause it to buy expensive EU imports (especially food and cars) rather than those from cheaper producers subject to EU tariffs. Britain's deficit is partly offset by its trade surplus with the rest of the world. Some Eurozone countries have permanent structural deficits with others, which the Euro system makes very difficult to adjust. Such surpluses and deficits are distorting and dangerous, and the Eurozone as a system is permanently fragile.[57]

The first disaster came in 2007–8, with a world financial crash. Because of its huge financial industry, Britain was exceptionally hard hit: after a period of growth that had made it the richest large country in Europe, its bank losses due to the crisis were equivalent to 20.9 per cent of GDP – more than three times the United States figure and nearly ten times the EU average. Over 700 City traders sold their Ferraris in a week.[58] But not using the Euro enabled the UK to stage a rescue operation, put together by the Bank of England and the Treasury. Banks were prevented from collapsing and depositors' money was guaranteed by the state to prevent panic. Sterling was allowed to fall to stimulate exports. Interest rates were brought right down, as the Bank of England began in 2009 creating vast sums of money and propagated a new euphemism – 'quantitative easing' (QE). Britain (and, because of the City's importance, the world financial system) thus avoided worse disaster because it still had its own currency: it was able, with the USA, to lead a global response to the crisis.

Eurozone countries were less fortunate. The European Central Bank (ECB) at first did nothing and then actually raised interest rates – 'wrong-headed decisions . . . because the ECB did not have to defend its position to anyone'.[59] The EU, led by Germany, refused to 'restructure' (that is, write off) some of the unpayable debts of its weaker members. This led to a second disaster: the Eurozone sovereign debt crisis, peaking in 2010–12, when the size of the debts incurred in the first crisis meant that several countries could no longer borrow. Greece, Italy, Spain, Portugal and Ireland were offered 'bailout' loans by the EU (increasing their indebtedness) but on condition – against basic economic sense – that they apply severe austerity measures: wage cuts, welfare cuts, job losses. This aggravated the damage and by shrinking their economies actually increased their burden of debt: Greece, for example, had government debt amounting to an already high 127 per cent of GDP in 2009, when austerity was imposed on it, but it rose to over 170 per cent as the economy shrank.

Ireland was forced to take loans from the IMF and EU, and, like Greece, was subjected to severe austerity supervised by the 'troika' (the European Commission, ECB and IMF). Irish politicians kissed the rod, and even backed harsh treatment of Greece – political Stockholm syndrome. Italians and Greeks protested through the ballot box, but election results between 2011 and 2015 were nullified: the EU threatened economic meltdown if they refused to take their medicine, and the elected politicians gave in or were removed.[60]

Unemployment, especially among the young, reached new heights and stayed there. The very existence of the Eurozone seemed periodically threatened by the prospect of a member state defaulting or leaving the Euro. No solution presented itself other than muddling through a succession of crises with last-minute improvisations, because while staying in the Eurozone was a disaster, trying to leave it threatened catastrophe.[61] Quantitative easing was only begun by the ECB *in extremis* in 2015 – six years after the UK. By the early 2010s the EU's popularity and legitimacy were falling in all but the most dependent countries. No British politician still espoused the official orthodoxy that the country should eventually adopt the Euro as a token of full participation in the 'European project'. It was now that UKIP began to take off electorally.[62] As Helen Thompson sums it up, 'the 2008 financial crash and the Eurozone crisis put a time-bomb under the sustainability of Britain's membership of the EU.'[63]

As Britain became the employer of last resort for southern Europe, clever, hard-working young people flocked to Britain, to the considerable improvement of the service sector, agriculture and some professions, if to the detriment of their home countries. Soon, hardly a restaurant in London was not staffed by pleasant and efficient young Romanians, Greeks and French. My college room was cleaned by a young Spanish woman with a business degree. Evidently something was wrong: people were being employed far below their qualifications. On the other hand, young and not-so-young British workers – not always as pleasant or efficient, and often indifferently educated and untrained – were being told, effectively, that no one needed them. It was not only the untrained who suffered, as international competition in many professions (including medicine and academia) greatly intensified. Britain was becoming a country of cheap, insecure labour and stagnant productivity.

After an inconclusive general election, a Tory–Liberal Democrat coalition took office on 12 May 2010, with David Cameron as prime minister. This was the first peacetime coalition since the last big economic crisis in 1931. Eurosceptics in the Tory party forced the government to pass a European Union Act (March 2011) requiring a referendum before any new power was given to 'an EU institution or body . . . to impose a requirement or obligation on the United Kingdom'. Cameron went further, in January 2013, promising that if he won the next general election (to be held in May 2015), he would negotiate an improved relationship with the Eurozone and subject it to an 'in–out referendum'. He saw this as a way of shutting up the Eurosceptics, who, for a generation, had dogged political leaders, and Tory leaders in particular.[64]

The Europe-wide elections to the European Parliament in May 2014 saw a surge of opposition to the EU almost everywhere outside Germany, mostly through anti-establishment parties of the Left and Right, and noticeably among young voters suffering from the economic slump. In Britain, UKIP topped the poll, while support for the Liberal Democrats, the most Europhile party, collapsed. A paper by the European Council on Foreign Relations in 2013 admitted that 'Euroscepticism . . . once seen as a British disease . . . has now spread across the continent like a virus . . . Everyone in the EU has been losing faith in the project.' Britain, once 'the Eurosceptic outlier', now looked like the leader of a growing trend.[65]

Nevertheless, there were and are significant differences between the British and their neighbours. Elsewhere, dissatisfaction with the EU sometimes means wanting it to be more effective, even more interventionist, at least for a substantial middle-class minority. But in Britain it means the opposite: 'less Europe' and even 'no Europe', rather than 'more Europe'. Opinion polls over the years have shown this consistently. If we look back before the post-referendum turbulence, the UK was the country in which fewest people (only 6 per cent) wanted more power to be given to Brussels; whereas in France and Spain, although more people than in Britain expressed 'unfavourable' views of the EU, over 30 per cent wanted it to be more centralized. Far fewer people in Britain (only 5 per cent) felt 'more European than national', and few wanted the EU flag to fly on public buildings – almost universal elsewhere. Britain, above all, was the only member state in which the majority felt more confident in facing the future outside than inside the EU.[66] This, surely, reflects the economic experiences of the previous generation, in which Britain no longer seemed 'the sinking Titanic', and even if it had been, the floundering EU was obviously no longer the 'lifeboat'.

The inescapable conclusion, well before the referendum brought the issue to the fore, was that people in Britain were not committed, emotionally or intellectually, to the 'European project', and that such was their settled view, confirmed repeatedly by opinion polls over the years. This seems not to have been clear to the political class, however. Despite the French, Dutch, Danes, Swedes, Irish and Greeks having all voted No in referendums in recent years, they were confident that they could persuade the most sceptical nation in Europe to vote Yes, wiping the floor with Eurosceptic 'head-bangers', and putting an end to the debate 'for a generation', perhaps for ever. Legislation for the referendum was supported by overwhelming majorities in both Houses, and by all parties. In proposing the Bill, the government made it clear that the decision was being given to the electorate, and it subsequently wrote to every household confirming that the vote would be authoritative. 'I say to the British people,' declaimed Cameron, 'this will be your decision.'

The plan was that his negotiations with the EU during 2015–16 would produce concessions on immigration, 'ever closer union' and economic guarantees as a non-Eurozone member sufficient to swing the vote. Polls suggested, indeed, that most people would want to stay in a 'reformed' EU with reduced powers.[67] But that was never on offer. This was not due solely to Cameron's failings as a negotiator, flagrant though they were. Britain's position outside the Eurozone gave it little leverage, and, moreover, the zone's financial crises had put immense pressure on Britain's position by increasing the desire of EU leaders to advance towards greater central control. Britain's semi-detached political and financial status (especially that of the City of London) was both less secure and less acceptable to its partners.[68] The dominant EU politicians saw no reason to make concessions or water down their own ambitions: Britain could accept them or leave. In February 2016 Cameron admitted 'the game was up'[69] for his strategy of tweaking the EU in Britain's interests. It was now plain that Britain had no significant influence within the EU – the dénouement of a forty-year illusion. The electorate had to choose not its preferred half-way house, but 'in or out'.

Could things have been different? Could the UK over the previous thirty years have emulated the single-minded determination of the French and muscled its way into a dominant triumvirate with France and Germany – arguably the logic of European power, and the key to achieving European integration?[70] Yes, in theory. But Britain's marginalization was due to its reluctance to force the pace towards economic and monetary union and a 'superstate' that most people in Britain and the rest of Europe did not want. As forcing the pace has so far proved both politically and economically destructive, Britain may have been right, both in its own interests and in those of Europe. But as most of Europe's political class disagreed, this meant that Britain's departure was probably only a matter of time.

The referendum campaign, which began in February 2016, was peaceful if excited.[71] Remain 'had the support of almost every entity with power in Britain, Europe, and the world from the senior civil service to the CBI to the big investment banks, to Obama and the world bureaucracy'.[72] There was one shocking act of violence, the vicious murder of the Labour MP Jo Cox on 16 June 2016, a few days before the vote. The murderer was a mentally disturbed loner obsessed with American and South African Nazis, but unconnected with any British group. He had apparently been waiting to kill someone for years, and the referendum provided the occasion.[73] This was the only act of serious violence of the whole Brexit period from 2016 to 2020 that can definitely be linked, however tenuously, to politics, though there was some aggressive behaviour on both sides.

When the British people voted on 23 June 2016, on 'Should the United Kingdom remain a member of the European Union or leave the European Union?', 51.9 per cent (of the 72.2 per cent who turned out) chose to Leave, compared with 48.1 per cent who voted to Remain: 17,410,742 people compared with 16,141,241. In a parliamentary election, this would have given a majority of 150, as nearly two-thirds of all constituencies voted to Leave.[74]

Two things are surprising and require further explanation. That the result caused so much astonishment; and that the majority was so small.

4. Divisions and Identities

'A gang of angry old men, irritable even in victory, are shaping the future of the country against the inclinations of its youth. By 2019 the country could be in a receptive mood: 2.5 million over-18-year-olds, freshly franchised and mostly remainers; 1.5 million oldsters, mostly Brexiters, freshly in their graves.'

Novelist Ian McEwen, urging a
second referendum, 2017[1]

'What they really want to do is kill democracy. They didn't like the answer they got before and so they'll just keep asking until people agree. As if we are all mindless morons.'

A north of England voter, 2018[2]

Reactions to the result were extraordinary, particularly in London and university towns: consternation, tears, anger, alarm. The EU, previously little loved, had somehow been 'transmogrified into the last best hope of humanity'.[3] Private opinion polls in Whitehall had predicted a comfortable Remain victory. David Cameron immediately announced his resignation. Even prominent Leavers seemed at a loss. Neither Nigel Farage nor Boris Johnson nor Michael Gove had expected to win. Johnson appeared dumbfounded, and his chance of becoming prime minister was ended by his main supporter Gove, who declared him unsuitable for office.[4] The two men most likely to lead a pro-Brexit government thus departed the field.

Who Voted and Why?

There was much overlap between the two sides: regions, socio-economic groups, sexes, ages, ethnicities, religions and occupations were all split. But there were considerable differences of weighting.[5]

The clearest divide was socio-economic. The pattern was by now familiar across Europe. Wherever and whenever people had been allowed to vote, the working classes and the less privileged – the excluded, the unemployed and simply the less well off – voted against the EU. In what has been described as 'probably the most directly class-correlated political choice' since the 1950s,[6] London was the only English region to choose Remain (59.9% of voters). Wealthy Kensington and Chelsea scored 68.7%, while in plebeian Barking and Dagenham only 37.6% agreed – strikingly close to the general European picture, where 71% of the elites but only 34% of the general public believed the EU benefited them.[7] Similarly, in the East of England (56.5% Leave): Cambridge voted to Remain (73.8%), while Peterborough, 30 miles away, voted 60.9% to Leave – a difference of 35%. An important marker of class was higher education: 57% of those with university degrees voted Remain.

The socio-economic difference was not solely a matter of income – a considerable minority of the middle-class voted Leave – but also of milieu and identity. The Remain vote was highly concentrated, so that a typical Remain voter might hardly know anyone who voted Leave.[8] Many Remainers were high earners, but there was also a big 'left-behind' element – university educated, economically struggling, often overqualified, feeling undervalued, politically marginalized and strongly present in the public sector – who were particularly likely to regard the EU as a protector of their interests and seem to have constituted the Remainer hard core. One commentator, describing this group as the 'everywhere precariat', even suggests that their 'European' cosmopolitanism is a compensatory fantasy.[9] In contrast, working-class identity, concentrated in certain regions, often included a strong national element. As the journalist Janice Turner puts it, 'The word "patriot" causes lips to curl on the London left where the Union Jack says imperialism, the England flag white nationalism. But elsewhere it means simply "we trust you".'[10] The economist Paul Collier points out that national solidarity is the bedrock of the rights of poorer citizens in Europe's nations.[11]

There was a decisive gender difference: men overall were strongly for Leave (55 to 45 per cent). While more privileged groups – those in business, the professions, university students – tended towards Remain, women in those groups, especially the youngest, were particularly pro-Remain.[12] An obvious explanation might be the well-documented willingness of men to accept perceived risk, whether crossing a road or leaving the EU.[13]

Also important was nationality. The Scots and the Northern Irish voted strongly for EU membership. In Scotland 1.6 million (62%) voted Remain to 1 million Leave (38%), a far higher rate of approval of the EU than on the Continent.[14] In Northern Ireland 440,000 voted Remain (55.8%) to 350,000 Leave (44.2%); and Irish citizens living in the UK, of whom over 500,000 had the vote,[15] were also presumably strongly for Remain. The reasons were clear. Scottish nationalists' hopes of independence relied on EU membership. For many Irish, common EU citizenship smoothed over the old North–South divide, and to nationalists like Sinn Fein it made unification of the island seem possible. England, and Wales almost to the same degree, were weighted towards Leave (53.4% and 52.5%), closer to general European feelings about the EU.

The youngest electors – the 18–24-year-olds – voted overwhelmingly to Remain, especially students (81 per cent); though non-students (many of them working class) were rather closer to the general picture. A majority of all over-45s voted to Leave. Much was made of this age difference by Remainers, who ascribed it to the greater openness and idealism of youth – though it might also be attributed to limited life experience and absence of responsibilities. More important was the anomaly of the British youth vote, which was never pointed out. Nowhere in Western Europe in June 2016 was youth support for the EU as high as in the UK. In countries where young people had suffered high unemployment as a result of Eurozone policies a bare majority was for the EU, or there was a majority against.[16] When faced with concrete choices at the ballot box, young voters regularly registered opposition: in the 2005 Dutch and French referendums, around 60 per cent of young voters in both countries opposed the proposed EU constitution, and in the 2015 Greek referendum, over 80 per cent of the young voted against its economic policies. When Emmanuel Macron stood as the only strongly pro-EU candidate in the French 2017 presidential elections, his support was lowest among young voters.[17]

In Britain, however, the same age group, especially its

student element, untouched by the chronic unemployment wrecking the lives of their European contemporaries, focused on the idealized cosmopolitan vision and a perceived threat to travelling and studying in Europe.[18] Relatively few of them actually do the latter: only 9,540 British students out of 2.3 million in higher education used the EU's Erasmus+ scheme in 2017–18; and of all British students studying abroad, 20 per cent more went to the Anglosphere than to the Continental EU.[19] It may be that the distinctive system of residential universities in Britain, reinforced by the loop effect of social media, created or reinforced homogeneity of opinion.[20] More broadly, there may be evidence that young people across the Western world, for whom not only the Second World War but also the Cold War are ancient history, may be less sensitive to issues of democracy and sovereignty,[21] and hence more attracted by transnational individualism. Or it could just be that people grow up: the youngest age group were similarly Europhile twenty-five years ago,[22] but by 2016 they had evidently changed their minds.

Ethnic minorities favoured Remain. Some, of course, come from the EU. But non-European minorities also supported Remain: 67% of Asians, 70% of Muslims, and 73% of Black voters.[23] Tower Hamlets, poor but with a high ethnic-minority population, voted like rich Kensington and Chelsea. There is incongruity in people of non-European heritage voting for an organization whose Eurocentrism in ideas and language is unabashed, and whose policies towards the developing world and migrants are less than exemplary – reasons why a sizeable minority, especially people of Indian origin, did indeed vote Leave.[24] But ethnic-minority support for Remain shows how little the EU itself was the issue for many voters. They seem instead to have been voting against a vision of an internal enemy: anti-immigrant 'right-wing Tories' and the middle-aged, male, white, provincial working class. In the tortuous world of 'intersectionality', the latter group inspires suspicion, even antagonism,[25] despite studies showing that every EU state is more racist than Britain.[26]

There was a sharper Left–Right division in attitudes to the EU in the UK than anywhere on the Continent, which may account for many of the above differences.[27] In Britain, the Left (Labour) and Centre-Left (Liberal Democrats, Greens), strong among young graduates and ethnic minorities, voted largely to Remain. Some on the British Left relied on EU legislation to carry out their aims rather than persuading the British electorate to do so, showing 'a pessimism about British politics'.[28] The Continental Left is less pro-EU, being more conscious of its policies as a source of unemployment and falling living standards; indeed, in Sweden, France and Greece the Left is more critical of the EU than is the Right. Yet one should not exaggerate the difference between the British and Continental Left: there were many working-class Labour Leavers (around a third of all its voters[29]) and a number of prominent Labour politicians and intellectuals were active Leavers, including the chair of the Vote Leave campaign. The Labour Party leadership tried, for a time successfully, to maintain a deliberately ambiguous position.

Analysis of the British vote shows that it was not as strange, and not indeed as 'British', as is generally supposed. At the time of the referendum, the percentage of people expressing a broadly 'unfavourable' view of the EU was very similar in the Netherlands (46%), Britain (48%), Germany (48%) and Spain (49%); far more took a negative view in France (61%) and, especially, Greece (71%). On economic policy specifically, many countries expressed greater 'disapproval' of the EU than the UK (55%), including Sweden (59%), Spain (65%), France (66%), Italy (68%) and Greece (92%).[30] A majority in France wanted a referendum on membership,[31] and President Macron thought they would 'probably' have voted to leave – or at least that a referendum would have been 'hard to win'.[32] More people in France thought the EU was bad for France (38%) than good (24%).[33]

From the 1990s onwards, as we have seen, increasing numbers of Europeans had begun to turn against integration. This showed itself first in negative or ambivalent votes on the Maastricht Treaty in France and Denmark in 1992, then on the Euro (Denmark in 2000 and Sweden in 2003 voted No), and again in the 2005 European Constitution referendums: in France, only professionals, the wealthiest districts of the Paris region, and overseas territories had strongly voted Yes – a prefiguration of the British vote eleven years later. Most recently, there had been No votes in Denmark (2015) and Holland (2016) on particular policies, and – more importantly – referendums or general elections in Italy and Greece (2015) had expressed mass opposition to the EU's economic policies. In February 2017, the Dutch parliament voted for an inquiry into the country's future relationship with the Eurozone, including possible ways of leaving it. The Danes have consistently opposed joining the Euro.

There was a broader pattern of quieter disaffection from the EU than occasional negative votes. Across Europe, the proportion of people expressing support for or trust in the EU, which had risen in the 1980s to a peak of nearly 80 per cent, had fallen sharply in the 1990s, and even more sharply since

2007, shrinking to only 40 per cent in 2013. There were fluctuations, but the trend and its cause were clear. Economic advantage now lay in countries shifting their trade outside the relatively stagnant Eurozone. Many people in their working lives must have realized the EU's diminishing contribution to their employment prospects and prosperity, hence they became less politically involved: Ashoka Mody has demonstrated that popular support for the EU itself follows the downward graph of intra-EU trade.[34] Confidence in the future viability of the EU has also declined.[35]

So the British, paradoxically, voted as typical Europeans. The simplest explanation for Brexit was this: the British had been given a vote, and, as the UK was not a member of the Eurozone, they could choose to quit the EU without the risk of financial meltdown. For a Eurozone country to leave the EU would be fraught with danger to the public finances and to private savings. The Greeks, the Italians and the French have all backed away from this. That risk would surely have been enough to ensure a Remain majority in the UK, as happened in the Scottish independence referendum of 2014 due to uncertainty over the currency.

Explaining 'Leave'

Whatever the similarities between British and Continental attitudes, there were nevertheless differences in feelings, myths and broad political identities. How important were they? Were we always destined to leave the EU because 'ever closer union' was incompatible with our long history? Brexiteers may like to think so, but the evidence is less than compelling. We voted in 1975 by a sizeable majority to stay in. If David Cameron had negotiated more successfully in 2015, it might well have tipped the balance towards remaining.[36] In 2016 we voted to leave by only a small majority, and a succession of polls over three subsequent years showed that the country was almost equally split. So, if European integration was indeed incompatible with our history, nearly half of us failed to realize it. Indeed, part of the country, and a powerful part, did all it could to cling to the EU, even at the risk of a constitutional crisis, as we shall see in the next chapter.

Nevertheless, commitment to the EU as a utopian vision, as a 'project', however attractive to some, was consistently lower in Britain than anywhere else (see above pp. 56–7). The obvious reasons are historical. Twentieth-century Europe experienced an unprecedented cycle of horrors: war, defeat, occupation, civil war, dictatorship, genocide and – perhaps no less corrosive – moral catastrophe and shame. General de Gaulle thought that France's leaders had 'sold its soul'.[37] How much more was this true of Germany – and not Germany alone. The idea of a united Europe therefore appealed not only to a longing for security and prosperity, but it drew a line under the past. Former dictatorships – Germany, Italy, Spain, Portugal, Greece – and newly liberated peoples of the communist bloc saw 'Europe' as a warrant of their emancipation and a safeguard against the return of historic nightmares. To be 'European' was to be free, decent and modern. That was worth paying a huge price for.

The twentieth century was experienced very differently in Britain. However great the trials, Britain had twice emerged victorious with a sense of national pride and vindication; and at the same time realized that it had survived with the support of countries outside a hostile or defeated Europe. For Britain, European integration had nothing to do with escaping past horrors – 'she felt no need to exorcise history', as Jean Monnet observed[38] – and everything to do with a sudden fear of a declining future, as we saw in Chapter 2. In 2013, only 16 per cent in Britain thought the EU meant 'peace', compared with 44 per cent in Germany.[39]

One could discuss which historical perception is more accurate. Sir Ian Kershaw, in his magisterial history of twentieth-century Europe,[40] ascribes post-war peace to the defeat of Germany 'once and for all', to the Cold War and superpower hegemony, to new prosperity, and to nuclear weapons – not, in short, to European integration. Ascribing peace and harmony to the EU is a matter of faith, not historical analysis. Fewer in Britain share it. Hence the EU enjoys far less moral lustre, and debate about it has been, and largely remains, utilitarian.

Another central theme of Britain's history diverts it from the idea of an inevitable European destiny. From the eighteenth century onwards, as summarized in Chapter 1, the new United Kingdom turned outwards. Consequently, Britain never became as economically integrated with the EU as its other members. Culturally and socially the British are highly 'connected' with Europe today,[41] but they are also more connected with the wider world. We can only guess at the psychological difference caused by having much of the world speaking our language, and of having long-established, non-European relationships such as those with the Commonwealth and the United States. The idea of 'global Britain' is simply more feasible and meaningful than would be (let us say) 'global Poland' or even 'global Germany'. The British 'have a bigger sense of abroad than most Europeans'.[42]

Finally, we have another historical narrative that carries great emotional power. Here, however, we need to be cautious. Brexiteers argued that attachment to parliamentary government and the practices of Common Law were inimical to membership of the EU, which may be objectively true.[43] But the history of the last four years shows that many of the principal guardians of these traditions, Members of Parliament and the Supreme Court, did not share this view, and indeed that historical claims about parliamentary sovereignty itself could actually be used to try to block or neuter Brexit. Moreover, while some EU states have limited democratic traditions, others (France, Italy, Poland, Hungary . . .) have histories of struggles for independence and democracy at least as proud as our own, but which so far they find compatible – if with some strain – with European integration: the price they pay to keep history at bay. Nevertheless, we do have a national story that has nourished Brexit. This we might call the 'Magna Carta tradition': the idea that when fundamental choices have to be made the people decide, and the rulers obey. Some of our European neighbours have very different national stories – what we might call a 'vanguard tradition'. France was shaped by monarchs, emperors and revolutionary minorities. Italy and Germany were created as single states in the nineteenth century, not by their peoples but by a few visionary ideologists and autocratic politicians: '*Fatta l'Italia, bisogna fare gli italiani*' ('We have made Italy, we must make Italians'), as one of them admitted. The people, if consulted at all, were merely summoned to endorse what their enlightened elites had done: active authority, passive democracy. This spirit animates the political practices of the EU. But it is not how the British instinctively think of their own politics.

Events since 2016 have emphasized the dogged determination of voters to be obeyed, whereas in several countries they have acquiesced in having their wishes repeatedly overruled. How much European irritation at Brexit is a result of this embarrassing contrast?

These historical peculiarities may be necessary to explain the Leave vote, but they are not sufficient. Had we been in the Eurozone, they might not have mattered, other than to nourish permanent discontent. As it was, they fostered a recognized and respectable ideological and political basis for Brexit within mainstream politics, ensuring considerable support within Labour and even among Lib Dems, Welsh nationalists and the SNP. In almost all other EU countries, radical opposition to the EU takes place on the extremes of Right or Left, which frightens off moderate voters. In Britain, although UKIP/ the Brexit Party provided a catalyst for the Brexit referendum, and subsequently a potent electoral weapon against both Tory and Labour Remainers, it was smoothly absorbed into a 'one-nation' Conservatism. So Brexit has taken place within the existing political institutions, and, indeed, has the potential to rejuvenate them – if they adapt to the new political situation.[44]

The 'Magna Carta tradition' is reflected in the way people described their reasons for voting in the Referendum.[45] Among Leave voters, the largest group (49 per cent – 8.5 million voters) said their main reason had been the principle that 'decisions about the UK should be taken in the UK'; and other reasons for Leave voting were similarly political. Behind this is both an emotional attachment to national sovereignty, and a range of other issues – most obviously immigration – which might be summed up as the hope that a British government outside the EU would pay more attention to voters' wishes.

Explaining 'Remain'

What requires explanation is less the Leave vote than the surprisingly large Remain vote. Remain voters said they were mainly motivated by economic considerations, principally that 'the risks of voting to leave the EU looked too great when it came to things like the economy, jobs and prices' (43 per cent). Nearly a fifth feared isolation – the old post-imperial declinism – but only 9 per cent claimed to be primarily motivated by 'a strong attachment to the EU and its shared history, culture and traditions'.[46]

Remain voters may, I suggest, be placed into four overlapping categories. First, Ideological Remainers. This small group (the aforementioned 9 per cent of Remain voters, about 1.4 million people) claim to be primarily motivated by an emotional commitment to the 'European project' – 'the last of the Enlightenment grand narratives'.[47] They support greater power being exercised by EU institutions, and some think of themselves primarily as 'Europeans'. For those sharing this sentiment (who seem from personal observation to include elderly as well as youthful idealists) the EU shares the same lineage as the League of Nations, the United Nations and even the Green movement. Whatever its shortcomings, they feel it somehow expresses 'peace on earth and goodwill to men'. It embodies European civilization in a traditional form – ancient Greece, the Renaissance, the Enlightenment – but 'shorn of its darker qualities'.[48] According to the philosopher John Gray, 'they think of themselves as embodiments of reason, facing down the ignorant passions of the unwashed rabble. But their rationalism is a vehicle for a dangerous myth, in which the EU is a semi-sacred institution.'[49] They may regard British and English national identity as outdated or even dangerous, and sometimes hold vehemently negative views of Britain and England – a considerable portion of this group, simple arithmetic suggests, may well be Scottish, Welsh or Irish nationalists.[50] Add to the mixture a strong dash of anti-Americanism and 'post-colonial guilt'. Such sentiments have a long pedigree, harking back to the late nineteenth and early twentieth centuries – in 1940 George Orwell mocked those who 'would feel more ashamed of standing to attention during "God Save the King" than of stealing from a poor box'.[51] This small Europeanist current was barely articulated in the referendum campaign, which had little to say about the EU or its future, yet it doubtless provided much of the vocal enthusiasm and activism of the post-referendum Remain movement.

The second category is 'Professional Remainers', whose common characteristic is commitment to membership of the EU through their careers and personal interests. For this, they cannot be condemned as long as their motives are open – like the Cambridge scientist who said publicly that 'Half of my postdocs come from Europe, my research funding comes from the EU, for me it's a no-brainer.'[52] This group includes executives of multinational companies, parts of the public sector, employees of lobby groups, NGOs, universities and think-tanks (especially the many that receive EU funding), employees of media organizations supporting Remain, businesses relying on EU immigrants, civil servants or diplomats accustomed to a high level of co-operation with EU institutions, and politicians representing Remain parties or constituencies or whose careers had been marked by strong support for the EU. As the journalist Simon Jenkins put it, rather acerbically, the EU 'had sent their children to Fontainebleau and Harvard, to apprenticeships at the World Bank and sinecures in a Brussels *cabinet*. Ever closer union had distanced them from their home countries and, fatally, from their electorates.'[53] This has been termed 'the withdrawal of the elites' into the EU, 'a protected sphere in which policy-making can evade the constraints imposed by representative democracy.'[54] For its adepts, familiarity with complicated EU systems and contacts in Brussels gave invaluable career advantages; conversely, Brexit posed a risk, indeed a humiliation. As one former diplomat put it:

> Our governing class – one might call them the progressive liberal consensus that encompasses a large chunk of MPs from the mainstream parties, senior civil servants, sections of the media, big business and their associated lobbyists – have suddenly found that their authority is under attack and their natural right to dictate the agenda called into question. And they don't like it.[55]

Of course, Professional Remainers might also be Ideological Remainers, but they are not necessarily so: 'The Government machine, the Commission, and the Cabinet Office were effective in scaring off prominent people from supporting us,' wrote Dominic Cummings; 'many of them told us (some embarrassed) about the phone calls they'd had and their "duty to shareholders" and so on.'[56] Professional Remainers were by far the most influential and powerful element in the Remain camp both before and after the referendum. Their arguments tended to be technical (such as the cost and complexity of leaving) rather than ethical. It is difficult to estimate the size of this group, though its size is of less consequence than its influence. Nevertheless, we may have a rough indication. The percentage of the British population who said before the referendum campaign that they thought the EU was an economic success was only 15 per cent, and those who thought that the EU was broadly 'going in the right direction' was only 20 per cent.[57] This total probably includes the Ideological Remainers. We might therefore roughly estimate Professional Remainers at around 10–15 per cent of the electorate. This group may share a 'managerial' rather than a 'populist' conception of politics and are likely to be risk averse.

The third category is 'Worried Remainers', the 43 per cent of Remain voters who were motivated by economic concerns. Before the referendum was called, only 15 per cent of the population, as noted above, thought the EU economy was doing well. Here we can surely see the effects of 'Project Fear' in inflating the Remain vote, not because of confidence in EU success but because of fear that leaving it would be worse. This is the largest and most malleable group, which almost tipped the referendum – roughly 7 million people, over 20 per cent of all who voted – and we shall return to it.

The fourth category might be called 'Status Quo Remainers', not enthused by the EU project, but who thought that Britain's semi-detached association gave it the best of both worlds. This attitude is easy to understand. For some people in fortunate countries not required to worry about the problems of the Eurozone, the EU offered tangible benefits, material and emotional. Some could choose to work abroad. Many middle-aged people (hundreds of thousands from the UK) could retire to sunnier and cheaper climes where they enjoyed the security of European citizenship and welfare systems. Emotional attachment to this 'Europe' is thoroughly understandable, as is the anger of many long-term expatriates at not being allowed to have their cake and eat it by voting in the 2016 referendum.

Did Remainers as a whole share any common assumptions? Did Leavers? For convinced Remainers, one is 'declinism': the belief that Britain is a much diminished and weak country, barely able to function economically or politically on its own. If for some this is a cause of alarm and regret,[58] many Remainers appear to cling to it gleefully, presumably as a way of repudiating the nation state, or at least the British nation state. The corollary is a *bien pensant* internationalism, whether as an ideal or merely as a convenience – ease of travel, and, for the better off, ownership of property in agreeable parts of the Continent. Such Europeanism (found in the richer parts of every EU country) can be costless: 'not . . . the acquisition of new obligations towards the less successful regions of Europe [but] the exit from former obligations towards the less successful regions of one's own nation'.[59] The problems facing the EU seem to cast little shadow: whereas post-Brexit Britain is confidently declared to be in terminal decline, the EU is assumed to be marching towards fulfilment and the resolution of its problems. 'The fantasy that another Europe is on the horizon,' comments John Gray, 'allows them to evade the mortifying truth that the European project belongs in the past.'[60] Here, surely, is 'nostalgia' – the trait they ascribe to Leavers.

Research suggests that being risk averse was an element in Remain voting. Although, judged rationally, standing still is not inherently safer than moving, clinging to the status quo is a common psychological response in referendums.[61]

Leavers were more confident in the country's capacities — perhaps more John Bull-ish — and less alarmist: poorer voters may have felt they had little to lose; older voters remembered that the time before the EU was hardly frightening; business people already trading outside the EU were untroubled.

Concern with immigration, and its effects on social cohesion, jobs, wages, housing, social services and simply on the character of the country, was clearly an important element of the wish to 'take back control': areas of very rapid immigration tended to vote Leave. The record high in net immigration came in 2015, and this surely added to the Leave vote. The worry was less immigration as such than its scale and uncontrolled character within the EU. This has long been a toxic issue in British politics, which does much to explain attacks on Brexit as 'racist', even though disquiet at large-scale immigration is found in all societies.[62] However, the idea that a deep and pre-existing cultural divide had been revealed by the 2016 referendum is an exaggeration. In their more general opinions and concerns, Remain voters were little different from Leavers (including UKIP voters) on political, social and cultural issues, including immigration, equality, ethnicity and national identity.[63] Immigration, for example, worried both sides: before the referendum, three-quarters of the population thought it had been too high and too rapid.[64] Yet there was a difference, at least among the more committed. Remainers gave more weight to economic issues and individual rights; Leavers, to family, community and national cohesion — a reflection of David Goodhart's distinction between 'Anywhere' and 'Somewhere' people. The latter 'still believe that there is such a thing as Society'.[65]

*

The referendum campaign itself was a frenetic and unedifying experience — 'Most of the "debate" was moronic as political debate always is.'[66] It did not decisively alter opinion, which, given the history of previous votes and polling in Britain and across Europe, was likely to favour leaving. Personally, I believed we might well vote to Leave when I saw the 2013 Eurobarometer finding that Britain was the only country in which a majority (53 per cent) believed they would be better able to 'face the future' outside the EU.[67] When the Leave campaign acquired two prominent figureheads, Boris Johnson and Michael Gove, I thought the result was probable. But the Leave campaign had to counteract the efforts of the Remain campaign, which included a government-backed tide of propaganda aiming to frighten voters into changing their minds.[68] With the aid of some rather desperate arguments, including Farage's scares about Turkish membership of the EU, and the notorious 'Boris bus', with its disputable claim to save £350 million a week, Leave narrowly held out.

What would the Leave majority have been if the Cameron government had remained neutral? Evidently more decisive. In 2005 it was believed that there would have been a 2 to 1 majority to reject the proposed EU Constitution. Similarly, in 2016, 65 per cent held Eurosceptical views, although half of these hesitated to take the decisive step of leaving[69] — an opportunity for Remain campaigners.

Economic Worries and 'Project Fear'

Consequently, the vote was close, and the next three-and-a-half years until Britain formally left the EU became

increasingly tense and angry, because so many people feared
the economic consequences of leaving. Were they right to do
so? Economic fear has become the tightest bond of the European Union. The Cameron government, in co-ordination
with the Remain campaign, from the outset made an un-
relenting effort to fan that fear, and under the May government
some ministers continued the same refrain in an effort to
mitigate what they saw as the disastrous referendum vote.
Cameron himself gave a succession of public warnings about
unemployment, pensions, farming, defence and the NHS.
The government drummed up battalions of business leaders
and marshalled a parade of foreign politicians to browbeat the
voters, including President Obama with his notorious warning that in future trade relations with the USA, post-Brexit
Britain would go to the 'back of the queue'.[70] Fear of American displeasure had been potent since the days of the Coal and
Steel Community. Not this time.

It was a calculated strategy. The biggest guns were Treasury forecasts of losses that would be caused by Brexit. These
were produced under George Osborne as chancellor: 'George
was using the formula of the Scottish referendum, where
the production of Treasury documents had really anchored
the No to Independence campaign.'[71] Given their status ('official
figures'; 'the government's own figures', etc.), these forecasts
were and still are repeatedly echoed, not only by Remain
campaigners and the media but by those 'experts from organizations with acronyms saying that they know what is best
and getting it consistently wrong', as Michael Gove put it.
Osborne heightened the fear by threatening an emergency
budget and tax rises, and both he and Cameron stated that a
Leave vote would cost every household £4,300.

The effect of this campaign was significant. Although groups such as 'Business for Britain' made counterarguments, and although some people took government statements with a pinch of salt, there were many who were alarmed – those the Downing Street opinion pollster called 'Hearts versus Heads': 'my heart says we should leave the EU but my head says that [it] is too risky.' Twenty-eight per cent of the electorate (largely my category of 'Worried Remainers') said they believed Osborne's warnings.[72] This surely reduced the substantial Eurosceptic majority in the country to a narrow majority for Leave. After the referendum, the same arguments were reiterated to try to neuter or reverse Brexit.

If 'Project Fear' was correct, then Brexit would cause – will still cause – major economic and financial damage over many years. If it was not, then the core of the Remain campaign, and the subsequent ill feeling and turmoil during the four years following the referendum, were based on error, if not deliberate scaremongering. This has serious implications for the honesty or competence of the politicians involved, and for the integrity of the civil service.

The Treasury's 200-page *Long-Term Economic Impact of EU Membership and the Alternatives* was published in April 2016. It forecast that future GDP growth would be lower in the long term under a 'clean' Brexit, and so households would suffer £5,200 in lost income after fifteen years. The analysis mainly depended on a 'gravity model', associating the amount of trade between any two countries with the size of their respective economies and the distance between them. The Treasury predicted devastating effects from tariffs, non-tariff barriers and administrative costs, causing exports to the EU to fall by half. The core of the analysis used statistics that were not even based on Britain's trade with the EU, but on the average for all EU members, which greatly exaggerated the importance of the EU for British exports, because (as we have seen) Britain traded less with the EU than any other member state. The Treasury assumed that these lost exports could not be replaced by other markets. It made big assumptions of the effects of 'uncertainty'. But the major element of the damage it forecast was a predicted decline in productivity caused by the assumed reduction in foreign trade. The evidence here was mostly derived from developing countries in the 1960s and 70s. Such countries did improve productivity through foreign trade; but in developed countries such as Britain there is no effect whatever. Yet this argument accounted for roughly half the Treasury's total predicted losses. By such calculations, it predicted that the UK would lose £36 billion a year in revenue.[73] Astonishingly, the Treasury itself had calculated in 2005 that the effect of EU membership on UK exports was only a small fraction of what they claimed in 2016.[74] Unusually, Treasury economists refused to discuss their workings with academic researchers.

A month before the referendum – carefully timed – the Treasury produced *The Immediate Economic Impact of Leaving the EU*. This stated unambiguously in a Foreword signed by Osborne that:

> a vote to leave would represent an immediate and profound shock to our economy . . . a recession . . . an increase in unemployment of around 500,000, GDP would be 3.6% smaller, average real wages would be lower, inflation higher, sterling weaker, house prices would be hit and public borrowing would rise.[75]

This alarmism was utterly disproved by events. There was no recession, and the UK economy grew by 1.8 per cent in both 2016 and 2017 – faster than the Eurozone. Unemployment actually *fell* by 280,000 over the next two years, and average wages rose.

These forecasts were endlessly recycled and even further exaggerated both before and after the referendum. Philip Hammond, the foreign secretary, drew on a statement made by the director general of the CBI, Carolyn Fairbairn (a zealous auxiliary of 'Project Fear') to assure the House of Commons that 'there would be almost a million fewer jobs in the UK by 2020 and that those under 34 would be hit the hardest.'[76] The vocal Remainer MP Heidi Allen told a meeting in her South Cambridgeshire constituency that 8 million jobs would be lost – a quarter of all jobs in the country, and sixteen times the already extreme Treasury estimate!

It would be tedious to go through all or even much of the endless reiteration of 'Project Fear', which continued unabated under the May government: for example, the leaked 'Cross-Whitehall Briefing' of January 2018, a simultaneous pessimistic report by the Scottish government, and the claim in June 2018 by the head of HM Revenue and Customs (part of the Treasury) that leaving the Customs Union would impose extra customs costs of £20 billion per year – a huge exaggeration, which had to be quietly withdrawn.[77]

What advice would voters have received if the Cameron and May governments had confined their officials to providing balanced information? We know, because there have been plenty of economic assessments by authoritative independent experts. Lord King, the former governor of the Bank of England, said that 'The idea that voting to leave would be an economic disaster doesn't match the facts . . . I don't believe that with adequate preparation, or in the long term, that the economic cost of leaving would be very different from staying in the European Union.'[78] The American Nobel Prize-winner Paul Krugman – a strong opponent of Brexit – criticized exaggerated forecasts of doom: 'sloppy thinking is always a vice, no matter what cause it's used for.'[79] Professor Ashoka Mody, the Indian former deputy director of the IMF's European department, accused the Bank of England of trying to outdo the Treasury in 'shrillness':

> their projected costs of exit have no basis in economic theory or empirical findings . . . When trade barriers between the UK and the EU go up, British producers will sell less to the EU and will sell more within the UK and to the rest of the world . . . although the transition costs are real, staying in the EU does not create obvious long-term economic and social gains.[80]

The exhaustive analysis of the Treasury forecasts by a team based at Cambridge found that it had demonstrably exaggerated, and that a reasonable conclusion would be 'that the effect of leaving the EU on economic growth, while negative, will be small'.[81]

Underlying these prudent independent assessments is an astonishing and counter-intuitive fact: there is no evidence that membership of the successive European communities has done anything at all to stimulate the UK's economic growth. Furthermore, this is true of most other countries, whether founder members or recent joiners. Twenty of the EU's members actually saw their growth rates fall after accession.[82] As was noted earlier (pp. 28–9), the dazzling economic success of the early EEC was due to post-war recovery and modernization, and, to a lesser extent, to one-off removals of high tariffs and trade barriers, also in the early years. By the time Britain joined, this was over. Since then, Europe has been a region of relatively slow growth, and the adoption of the Euro slowed it further. The EU is not only about economics, but that has always been its main selling-point. Yet the cupboard has long been bare.

A reasonable view therefore is that the medium-term economic effects of Brexit – if they can be reliably estimated at all – are small, whether positive or negative, and the long-term effects – even more difficult if not impossible to estimate – depend largely on the policies followed by post-Brexit governments. On that subject, there was, as Remainers reasonably pointed out, considerable disagreement or uncertainty among advocates of Leave, who covered a wide political and intellectual spectrum. Some made predictions as extravagantly positive as their opponents' were extravagantly negative.

For that reason, as most Leave voters sensed, this was essentially a political, not an economic, decision. Dr Paul Sheard, the Australian former vice-chairman and chief economist of the global ratings agency Standard & Poor's and a senior fellow at the Harvard Kennedy School, believes that

> Brexit is not really about economics; it is more about national identity and enough British citizens deciding, when given the choice, to take back part of the sovereignty they had previously ceded to the EU . . . I think that the longer term (5–10 year horizon) challenges are likely to be more serious for the EU27 than for the UK.[83]

Professor Ashoka Mody, now at Princeton University, takes a similar view: 'On Brexit, British citizens and their leaders must decide what kind of nation they want to live in,' and not use 'frightening economic scenarios' to distort the debate.[84]

Narratives of Leave and Remain

We spent several years trying to make these decisions about identity, sovereignty and the kind of nation we want to live in, and, until the COVID crisis, we had not managed to agree. Families and friendships were strained. 'Leave' and 'Remain' replaced other political banners, like the Greens and Blues in Byzantium: by mid-2019, 88 per cent of the public identified with one side or the other, and 72 per cent did so strongly or fairly strongly.[85] Two opposing narratives emerged. The Leave narrative – what David Goodhart has termed 'decent populism' – focused on democracy and national sovereignty, seen as being under attack from self-interested and even treacherous elites – politicians, judges, lobbies. The main argument was that the people had decided, and their vote must be respected.

The Remain narrative, perhaps naturally for the losing side, was even more vehement, arguably as 'therapy'.[86] Its starting point – which proved impenetrable to argument – was that the Leave vote was simply perverse. It had therefore to be discredited, explained away, and set aside. The narrative featured one absence, one paradox and one trope. The absence was the EU: rarely discussed and hardly ever analysed. The paradox was insularity: 'Europhiles' seemed oblivious to attitudes and developments on the Continent. The trope was that Leave was essentially about Englishness: its nostalgia, xenophobia and failure. The narrative could therefore concentrate on a horrified contemplation of the awfulness of the English. That Scotland, Northern Ireland and London had voted Remain was important to the Remainer narrative, as it reinforced the Englishness trope, spiced with the traditional Anglophobia of Scottish and Irish nationalism.[87] Hence, Scotland was progressive, 'open', 'European' and morally superior to England; London was modern and cosmopolitan, practically a separate country; England in contrast was provincial, bigoted and 'left behind'.

All was not as it seemed, however. Scottish attitudes towards the EU were similar to those in England: 60 per cent of Scots could be classified as 'Eurosceptic' in 2015, they lacked any 'gut attachment to European identity', and their views on immigration were similar to those in the UK as a whole.[88] The difference was the nationalist ambition for independence, feasible only within the EU. Given the unanimous calls to vote Remain from the Scottish establishment, one Scottish observer found it 'surprising' that a third of Scots (including many SNP supporters) voted to leave.[89] London was indeed dynamic, vibrant, diverse and exciting to visit. It was also highly unstable, uniquely unequal socio-economically, on average worse off than the rest of southern England, racially polarized, with a constantly churning population, little sense of community, many struggling young people, and the lowest life-satisfaction levels anywhere in the country.[90] Londoners were unlikely to be swayed by appeals to national solidarity and sovereignty: their vote split more deeply along class and ethnic lines than anywhere else in Britain.

Those horrified by the Leave vote produced a range of

arguments to discredit it. The issue was too complex for the electorate to decide by 'in—out referendum' (though this is what Parliament had chosen when it thought Remain would win). It was too difficult, some declared, for democracy itself: when the wrong people formed the majority it was mere 'populism' — even 'among the worst of the current world-wide horde of nationalist populisms'.[91] Leavers were ignorant ('low-information'), poor ('left behind'), bigoted, and gullible dupes of the tabloid press, the Russians, Cambridge Analytica,[92] the notorious bus, and 'silver-tongued demagogues such as Boris Johnson and Michael Gove'.[93] Moreover, they were old: depriving the young of their promised land, 'driven by nostalgia for a world where passports were blue, faces were white and the map was coloured imperial pink'.[94] Many would soon die, so the vote was invalid, and should be cancelled or re-run. If both sides sometimes used inflammatory language, only that attacking Leave voters was biological.

A slew of ephemeral political tracts and op-ed columns furnished variations on the trope of English perversity, which would bring down economic fire and brimstone on the heads of the very people who had voted badly.[95] The commonest characteristic of Remainer polemics was a refusal to acknowledge Leave as a legitimate political decision; Remainers understood Leavers far less than Leavers understood them.[96] Voting Leave, they thought, must be a psychological aberration, an irrational fantasy (like voting that the earth was flat[97]), a primitive atavism that 'reaffirms the tribe's ancestral values against a disappointing modernity', like 'the Xhosa . . . killing cattle and burning crops [in a] self-destructive quest for riches and freedom'.[98] In a book relished by Remainers, an Irish journalist, Fintan O'Toole, saw 'the Brexit psychodrama' as a product of 'the English reactionary imagination', whose 'deep pulse' was 'the political erotics of imaginary domination and imaginary submission'.[99] One Oxford professor wrote a book explaining Brexit as 'the anguish of losing an empire and the fantasy of recovering it', and another wrote of 'English post-imperial delusions of grandeur'.[100] Two other academics (perhaps the only people to blame Brexit on 'a patriotic BBC') vouchsafed the thought that 'the [recent] years of the long recession have brought with them a nostalgia for a time when life was easier, and Britain could simply get rich by killing people of colour and stealing their stuff.'[101] Commented John Gray, 'Among all the embarrassingly hackneyed investigations of the post-imperial English psyche . . . that litter the liberal media, you will struggle to find any reference to the dark forces that are shaping European politics.'[102] Richard Tuck noted that the social groups most strongly for Leave had, in the past, been the least interested in or supportive of the Empire. He suggested that the boot was really on the other foot: it was the EU that was underpinned by 'imperial nostalgia', as an 'alternative stage upon which these old imperial ruling classes could regain something of the role they had lost, making lives (as they thought) better for populations who had no direct say in how they were being governed'. Brexit, on the contrary, was 'in reality a desire for a final emancipation from the burden of empire'.[103]

Remainers jealously claimed a monopoly of internationalism, even while crouching behind the EU's heavily guarded borders. So they made accusations to all and sundry that the Brexit vote was a xenophobic spasm. Two episodes became the subjects of sensational comment nationally and abroad. One was the daubing of a slogan on a Polish cultural centre in

Hammersmith immediately after the referendum. The other was the death shortly afterwards of a Polish man, Arkadiusz Jóźwik, in Harlow. The BBC referred to 'a frenzied racist attack triggered by the Brexit referendum'; the *Guardian* declared that the death 'exposes the reality of post-referendum racism'. The president of the EU Commission, Jean-Claude Juncker, said, 'we Europeans can never accept Polish workers being harassed, beaten up or even murdered on the streets of Harlow.' The Hammersmith daubing turned out to be a slogan attacking the OMP, a Polish Eurosceptic think-tank that supported Brexit.[104] The death was an accident during a drunken brawl apparently started by the victim, and the trial found no evidence of xenophobia.[105] Truth did not muffle the chorus of loathing. I heard prominent British Remainers on public platforms in both France and Italy months and years later repeating these stories and asserting that Britain was racked by 'hate crime'.*

The print media were divided. The business press was adamantly anti-Brexit, as were Left-liberal and pro-Labour papers, both broadsheet and tabloid. Conservative papers mostly went the other way, though *The Times* oscillated in the middle. There were also divided views within the same newspapers, both about Brexit generally and about particular government policies. The BBC was accused by both sides of favouring the other, which it habitually takes as proof of rectitude. But its Remain sympathy, which could not but shape language and perceptions, was measurable. The *Today*

---

* Hate crime is rare and has been falling over the last decade; its typical victims are not EU citizens, but young Muslim men, especially following terrorist incidents. Home Office, 'Hate Crime, England and Wales, 2017/18', *Statistical Bulletin* 20/18, 16 October 2018.

programme's business news from June to December 2016, for example, featured 366 guest speakers, of whom 52 per cent were negative about the Leave vote, and 16 per cent positive. Not a single BBC programme examined the potential benefits of Brexit.[106]

Reactions to the referendum vote abroad largely echoed those at home. The international political, business and media classes were outraged: the *New York Times*, *Le Monde* and so on took their tone and content from the *Guardian*, the *Financial Times* and *The Economist*. There were sympathetic voices, and some even applauded, particularly in Australia, New Zealand and the United States. The Australian elder statesman John Howard wrote: 'I hope that British leaders will see the special endowments of history, language and past associations that their country has with the growth areas of the Asia Pacific as the vehicle for new and expanded economic links.'[107] Another Australian leader let it be known privately that he regretted having let himself be dragooned into publicly opposing Brexit by David Cameron. Donald Trump's support, when it came, was welcome though embarrassing. But the official tone was, overall, disapproving: the British (or English) had disgraced themselves, and were unfit for the brave new 'rules-based' world.

Culture Wars?

What might loosely be termed the intelligentsia, from actors to academics, participated volubly in the national quarrel. They were overwhelmingly Remain (nearly 90 per cent of academics, for example[108]): reassuring to Remainers that they were obviously right; annoying to Leavers who felt they were being betrayed; but in any case strangely monochrome for a group whose stock in trade is original thought.

Some bemused writers ventured north of Watford to explore darkest England, one on a bicycle.[109] James Meek set himself to understand 'dreams of leaving and remaining', but he could not escape the cast-iron assumption that Remainers were rational and Leavers just deluded. Revealingly, when a farmer told him that Brexit might damage farming but 'there are more important things than farming', he could not understand.[110] His own Remain dream was backpacker cosmopolitanism — 'being at once an element in a vast, variegated, rich continent, and losing myself in wanderings'.[111] Anthony Barnett, the founder of Charter 88, published the most substantial and original Remainer treatise — original not least for being more than a diatribe, discounting 'Project Fear', criticizing 'today's EU' ('a thief in the night, created in defiance of popular consent') and understanding the democratic motive of Leavers. Yet he still assumed Leave was an internal English pathology, and favoured Remain in the hope of a democratic revolution within the EU.[112] Timothy Garton Ash eloquently expounded a romantic 'Ideological Remainer' vision: a 'shared destiny', a 'battle for Europe' against 'the global tide', with 'a European England' supported by 'millions of British Europeans and EU citizens living in Britain' — a 'democracy fighting back', presumably against its own unenlightened majority.[113]

Academics, led by massed vice-chancellors, typically spoke of their corporate interests, not of the interests of society. Much was said about EU research funding, although the UK contributes more than it receives, as Sir Noel Malcolm worked out from the (rather elusive) official statistics – a finding that the University of Cambridge repeatedly declined to publish.[114] One prominent left-wing intellectual remarked that 'at Cambridge, the Vice-Chancellor's office censored unwelcome opinion with stone-walling worthy of the Writers' Union under Brezhnev.'[115] Institutional pressure made many Leavers, especially younger academics with vulnerable careers, cautious about speaking out.[116]

The stifling consensus produced some works better passed over in silence, and a few of real interest. Among the latter, three historians – David Reynolds, Brendan Simms and Stuart Sweeney – gave reasoned support to the Remain cause, all relating the long relationship of the British Isles and the Continent.[117] A fourth historian (the present writer) traces the same story briefly in Chapter 1 of this book. We all emphasize the importance of this relationship but reach different conclusions. Reynolds regrets Brexit on the orthodox Remainer ground that Britain is thereby weakened and marginalized, and he sees the problem as stemming from the failure to get involved in integration in the 1950s. Simms, writing before the referendum, feared Brexit on opposite grounds: that the loss of Britain ('the last European Great Power') and its influence ('fundamentally different and more benign') is disastrous for European security and for the European project itself. Sweeney discusses the forces he believes make European unity necessary, even inevitable – an interesting but risky combination of determinism and British declinism. I think they all underestimate the transformation brought about by Britain's three-century relationship with the world outside Europe, which (noted another historian) 'reinforced the advantage of an island position: namely, that one is not tied by nature to others that one would not choose to have as neighbours.'[118] They also underestimate the fissiparous tendencies within the EU (discussed in Chapter 3), now approaching a critical stage. This is characteristic of Remainer writing, including a detailed and lively Brexit history by an economic historian, Kevin O'Rourke, son of a former Irish ambassador to London, who effectively skewers the pathetic thrashings of the May government, but appears to believe that Messrs Barnier and Varadkar were embodiments of reason and moderation and that the Leave vote had nothing to do with EU failings.[119] Those failings are dissected by another economic historian, Ashoka Mody, in his authoritative and devastating history of the Euro.[120]

Novelists too entered the fray, but had disappointingly little to say. Ian McEwan dashed off a slight and unfunny satire. Julian Barnes distilled Remainer clichés, deploring Britain's 'deluded, masochistic departure from the European Union'. Ali Smith and Kate Atkinson dropped anti-Brexit asides into novels about other things. Atkinson made the villains in *Big Sky* Brexiteers, although their business (sex trafficking Eastern Europeans) would logically make them enthusiasts for Free Movement. Jonathan Coe's *Middle England* ('Brilliant' – Nicola Sturgeon) was a nostalgic satire in which nice people were Remainers and Brexiteers were old, bigoted and manipulated by sinister forces; it ended on a cheerful note as Brexiteers died and nice people fled Birmingham for sunny Provence and 'an endless supply of red wine'. A rare literary foray from the other side, Julie Burchill's comic play about Remainers, *People Like Us*, was booked out at the Union Theatre but panned by the critics.

Intellectuals who publicly supported or accepted leaving

were fewer. The conservative philosopher Roger Scruton prioritized culture, community and nation, 'a society held together by trust between strangers', the bedrock of tolerance, democracy and inclusivity. He regretted that many Remainers seemed animated by 'repudiation of home – the turning away from the inherited first person plural', and he argued that Britain always had been and remained part of true European culture.[121] John Gray, also a philosopher, wrote mordant political commentaries, one of which identified the 'fellow-traveller' mentality attractive to intellectuals: 'The ease with which fellow-travellers pass over the casualties of the regimes with which they identify is one of their defining traits . . . They are attracted by any large political experiment that seems to prefigure a new order of things.'[122] Richard Tuck, a left-wing historian of ideas, provided incisive analyses of the politics, as did the economist Graham Gudgin of the economics.[123] Matthew Goodwin attempted to explain 'populism' rather than abusing voters.[124] Chris Bickerton provided a critical inside analysis of the EU system, in which former nation states were reduced to dependent 'member states'.[125] Vernon Bogdanor, a leading constitutional expert, hoped that Brexit, 'a new beginning', might catalyse constitutional reform.[126] Paul Collier, an economist who had voted Remain but accepted Leave, reflected on the growing importance of community and the need for an 'economics of belonging' through which post-Brexit policy must redress the inequalities created by the globalized metropolitan culture of 'individual rights and group privileges'.[127] Stephen Davies wrote a detailed political analysis, arguing that Brexit marked a fundamental realignment of political forces in Britain and Europe.[128] Several of these writers drew on the most seminal work published in the wake of the referendum, David Goodhart's analysis of 'Some-where' and 'Anywhere' people, which is not solely about Brexit, though its arguments substantiate Leave as necessary for 'a new settlement' in Britain.[129]

Many prominent Remainers assumed an intellectual and moral superiority over their opponents, whom they endlessly dismissed as ignorant, xenophobic and nostalgic. Yet their own arguments were nullified by an elementary intellectual fallacy: ascribing Brexit to British or English exceptionalism. 'Brexit is at heart an English nationalist project,' declaimed Timothy Garton Ash. 'The flag of St George, the language, the mystique, the emotional appeal of England and Englishness have been misappropriated by nationalists and xenophobes.'[130] Their blindness to the general European disillusionment with a system that was fundamentally undemocratic and dis-astrously failing is incomprehensible. Their concerns were understandable. But the monotonous pessimism with which they expressed them betrayed an ungenerosity of spirit towards the majority of their fellow countrymen, whom they hardly seemed to know and to whom they willingly ascribed the worst of motives. People proud of their open-minded cosmopolitanism seemed unable to sympathize with their neighbours.

If intellectuals are meant to enrich and enlighten public debate, this was not their finest hour. The two sides could not really engage. They did not share the same logic, the same understandings of the present and the past, or the same loy-alties. What to one side was a corrupt and unaccountable bureaucracy to the other was an inspiring vision of the future; what to one side was treachery to the other was enlightened cosmopolitanism; what to one side was patriotism to the other was nostalgia or xenophobia. They barely spoke the same language, and most did not try.

Did Brexit show the existence of a deep and bitter cultural divide splitting the country down the middle? To some extent yes: a mixture of class, gender, age, interest and milieu created somewhat different views of the world. The tone of the debate was coarsened and polarized by the most ideologically committed minorities on both sides (the 'global villagers' and the 'hard authoritarians'[131]), who really did represent conflicting cultures. Convinced Remainers were over-represented in the media, politics, academia and the arts, which gave them ample opportunity to stoke controversy. But Paul Collier suggests that the divide was not as wide as it seemed: if Britain had been outside the EU and its people had been asked in 2016 if they wished to join, the answer would have been 'an overwhelming consensus for "out".'[132] Moreover, as noted earlier, in general attitudes there is no great divergence between most Leavers and Remainers. The Brexit controversy did not expose a previously unrecognized gulf between two nations: it opened one. The close result of the referendum, the alarm whipped up by 'Project Fear', and then more than three years of uncertainty, agitation and polemic – the subject of the next chapter – combined to heighten emotions and create for a time a real sense of national crisis.

5. Stopping Brexit – Almost

'Il ne peut y avoir de choix démocratique contre les
traités européens.'
>
> Jean-Claude Juncker, president of the European
> Commission, January 2015

'A few weeks after the Brexit referendum, I went out in
the evening with a friend . . . a small 'l' liberal . . . well-
travelled, open-minded, Oxbridge-educated . . . "I don't
get it," he said. "What about all these powerful backroom interests in the City that are supposed to have the
government in their pocket? Why aren't they stepping
in behind the scenes to stop this?" '
>
> James Meek, 2019[1]

During the three-and-a-half turbulent years that followed the
referendum, the confusion around various shades of 'soft' and
'hard' Brexit slowly cleared as negotiations between London
and Brussels sank deeper into the mire. There was only one
meaningful Brexit, which was to leave the Single Market, the
Customs Union and the jurisdiction of the European Court of
Justice, but there were many forms of non-Brexit. One was
blunt: to overrule the referendum, which eventually became
the position of the Liberal Democratic Party. More prudent
was to demand another referendum, usually on the grounds
that 'we know much more now' – seemingly oblivious to the
fact that remaining in the EU also carried unknown risks.

Other tactics were more subtle: to proclaim that formally the United Kingdom would no longer be a member of the EU, but to conclude a net of agreements that would keep it as an associate, obeying EU laws, adhering to EU policies and perhaps, in time, returning sheepishly to the fold – an outcome, some argued, that better reflected the divided opinion of the country. This was officially termed an 'ambitious, broad, deep and flexible partnership'. But compromise proved elusive, partly because of the divisions within the UK discussed in the previous chapter, and partly because of the unyielding attitude of the EU.

At stake was sovereignty, a term often used but rarely discussed. At its simplest, sovereignty is the right to make the final political decision, and to be obeyed. In recent decades it has been common to talk of sovereignty being 'shared' or 'pooled' through international laws and organizations. This seems to me a misunderstanding. Certain powers may be delegated for a time to others, but sovereignty, the ultimate right to decide, can exist only within a political community: it can be given up, but not shared. The sovereignty that may have seemed an abstract concept suddenly became real after 2016, when two fundamental questions arose. First, was the United Kingdom still a sovereign state? Second, if it was, who or what was sovereign within it?

On the first question, the UK, through a legally enacted referendum, had voted to leave the EU – a clear act of sovereignty. But would it really carry out that decision, or would it be pressured into abandoning it? Whatever the legal theory, if it gave in to pressure, it would have ceased in practice to be a sovereign state for the indefinite future, for sovereignty that cannot be exercised is sovereignty lost: as Thomas Hobbes put it, 'he that deserteth the Means, deserteth the Ends.'[2] By this criterion, some EU member states (most obviously Greece, Ireland and Italy, and perhaps others where popular votes have been overruled) have given up their sovereignty. Perhaps, indeed, they all have. President Macron frequently talks of 'a sovereign Europe'.[3] He may be right.

On the second question, who within the state – institutions, groups, persons – actually makes the final decision? Within democratic states, sovereign authority is divided up by the separation of powers, and it is rarely if ever necessary to ask who or what is the ultimate sovereign. In the UK, the legal sovereign is 'the Crown in Parliament' – an enigmatic hybrid. But there is potentially a difference between legal theory and political reality. If the state ever broke down, we would find out who could really act and be obeyed: the monarch, the prime minister, Parliament, the Supreme Court, the armed forces, or some combination. Fortunately, we have not approached such breakdown for over three centuries, but we did see in 2019 an attempt by Parliament, and especially the House of Commons, to claim sovereignty for itself – even if, by a crowning irony, its aim was in effect to cede that sovereignty to the EU by nullifying the referendum decision to leave.[4]

Had the House of Commons succeeded, Britain would have been, as a majority of MPs clearly preferred, a participating member of an embryonic European federation. But it would not have been a sovereign democratic nation. The uncertainty was ended by a reassertion of sovereignty by the entity that ultimately holds it in a democracy – the people. The referendum vote was confirmed by a series of elections. Some considered this alarming, even un-British: the irruption of direct popular democracy into a long-established parliamentary system. Yet the constitution and the law itself were regarded by the great seventeenth- and eighteenth-century legal authorities Hale and Blackstone as founded on popular custom – 'the wisdom of unlettered men', in Edmund Burke's famous phrase. If this is partly myth, decisive popular participation in crucial political acts has undoubtedly been part of our history since time immemorial. As Roger Scruton has written, 'For us, political choices are underpinned by the sovereignty of the people, mediated by Parliament and the Common Law.'[5] The Glorious Revolution of 1688 included numerous meetings of citizens, sometimes bearing arms, ready to enforce the popular will with more than words if need be. The Great Reform Act (1832) was forced on Parliament by popular tumult. So, to a certain degree, was women's suffrage – the completion of democracy. Parliament has been instrumental in great decisions, but by mediating – in Scruton's term – as the voice of the national community, not separate from or independent of it, and certainly not as its superior.

Immediately after the referendum, some naïve Leave supporters seem to have thought that the question had been decided and that the UK would simply 'walk away'. Cameron during the referendum campaign had promised (or threatened) to notify the EU of Britain's departure as early as 24 June in the case of a Leave vote. But his government had deliberately made no plans for leaving[6] – the same *politique du pire* adopted at the time of the Scottish referendum. So there was no Brexit policy. Would the UK in future be a 'third country' trading under World Trade Organization rules? Would it try to remain in the Single Market and/or the Customs Union? Would it aim at the 'Norway Option' of associate status, or seek to renew its membership of the European Free Trade Association or the European Economic Area? Would it negotiate something 'bespoke' with the EU, and if so, what and how? The enigmatic Theresa May became prime minister on 13 July. She had been an unemphatic Remainer, and consistently refused to express personal support for Brexit. She now assumed a formidable burden, if not a poisoned chalice. Her Cabinet carefully included Remainers (notably the chancellor of the exchequer Philip Hammond) and Leavers (including Boris Johnson as foreign secretary and Michael Gove as environment secretary).

It soon became clear that a substantial number of Remain supporters (estimated at 10–20 per cent of the electorate[7]) did not accept the referendum verdict. Campaigners were prepared to use unprecedented political and legal methods to overturn it. A newspaper, *The New European*, was founded in July, and Tony Blair used it to urge Remainers to 'mobilize and organize' to stop Brexit; it later acquired Alastair Campbell, Blair's former spin doctor, as editor-at-large. The official Remain organization rebadged itself 'Open Britain' in August, and its meetings took place in Blair's offices. The Liberal Democrats demanded a repeat vote. Gina Miller, a businesswoman who thought Brexit was 'one of the most extreme rightwing experiments we have witnessed since the 1930s',[8] funded a legal challenge to the government's right to notify the EU of the UK's intention to leave under Article 50 of the Treaty of Lisbon. Assuming that EU members were still sovereign states, this was a question of inter-state relations, and hence of executive (in Britain, royal) prerogative. The Miller challenge disputed this, and both the Divisional Court and the Supreme Court ruled in January 2017 that Parliament would have to legislate for the government to give notice under Article 50 – the first time such a necessity had ever been suggested. It was a contentious ruling, arguably shaped by politics, and a dissenting judgment of the Court argued that it was wrong in law.[9] There was little immediate practical effect, however, as Parliament duly voted on 8 February, by 494 to 122, to trigger Article 50, and May gave the official notification on 29 March 2017, meaning that the UK would leave on 29 March 2019. But the judgment showed that the legal foundations were shifting, that established law and constitutional practice were vulnerable, and that more challenges to the executive were likely. For the moment, however, most people (55 per cent to 19 per cent) trusted May.[10]

In contrast, three-quarters of MPs,[11] and most officials advising ministers and conducting negotiations with their European counterparts, disapproved of Brexit. The Leave vote, said the ardent Remainer Lord Adonis, had caused 'a nervous breakdown' in the civil service. It was reported that 'the view in Whitehall is that, of the 40 or so permanent secretaries, only one voted for Leave'.[12] Either they were convinced of British weakness, which made it a supplicant ('We will huff and puff but, in the end, we will basically come to heel'[13]). Or they simply believed that EU membership – or the most that could be salvaged – was in the nature of things. Few could remember when this had not been so. Many in all departments had spent their careers within the EU orbit: they were 'Professional Remainers' par excellence, averse to unpredictable change.

A reiterated argument was that the European Union was an immense entity 'of 500 million people', whereas the United Kingdom was only a 'small offshore island'. The EU was 'the world's largest market', on which Britain was dependent and whose terms it had no choice but to accept: otherwise we would run out of food and medicine, lorries would queue for miles both to leave and to enter the country, and 'millions' would lose their jobs. True, a majority had voted to Leave, but, as a Remainer catchphrase had it, 'no one voted to become poorer', and so wiser heads must save them from their folly. A leading Remainer wrote gleefully that 'Theresa May will have to take pretty much whatever medicine she is given in Brussels . . . Drink up, Theresa'[14] – an interesting echo of the 'swallow the lot' mentality of the early 1970s.

The relationship between the UK and the EU could be described in very different terms, however. In both 'hard' and 'soft' power Britain was the leading EU state.[15] Economically, it was equal to the eighteen smaller members of the EU: it is as if Brexit reduced the EU from twenty-eight members to ten. Most British trade was with only six of them: the rest of 'the world's largest market' was largely irrelevant. Moreover, as noted earlier, Britain's trade with the EU has been diminishing in importance for two decades. The Continental countries with which we trade significantly – Germany, France, Italy, Holland and Belgium – collectively enjoyed a huge trade surplus with the UK (£70 billion in 2019), which would, if interrupted or reduced, cause them serious economic damage.[16] Britain was as large a market for German goods as China. Moreover, Britain was the most profitable market in the world for both Germany and France: Germany had a trade surplus with Britain of €46 billion, and France a surplus of €12 billion, which helped to balance its €32 billion deficit with the EU as a whole.[17] The goods that Britain imported (notably cars and food) were potentially subject to high tariffs, which would encourage consumers to turn to British or non-EU suppliers. A German academic study estimated in 2019 that France could lose 50,000 jobs and Germany 100,000.[18] But the services that Britain exported were not subject to tariffs, and there were no alternative suppliers of some of the most important of them – the City of London's specialized financial services. Early alarms that large parts of the City would decamp to Paris, Frankfurt or Dublin if denied 'passporting rights' soon proved hollow – most of its business did not need 'passporting' anyway. If the UK abolishes most tariffs on its global trade, its losses from Brexit have been estimated as small, and less than those of the EU.[19]

In short, though the EU was indeed much bigger than the UK, and although the UK was more dependent on the EU than vice versa, the imbalance was far less than pessimists made out, and the negotiating position less one-sided. But May and her officials seem not to have seen things thus. From the beginning, they accepted the EU's rules for negotiation, even though these arguably contravened the Lisbon Treaty: they agreed that matters the EU was interested in should be prioritized, and that progress in the negotiations should therefore be controlled by the EU. One of its priorities was the large financial contribution ('divorce bill') it demanded on the grounds that the UK had agreed to a range of future expenditure while a member, and although this was logically and legally contestable[20] the government agreed to it almost from the outset.

Mrs May set up two new departments of state. The inelegantly named Department for Exiting the European Union (DExEU), under David Davis, and the Department for International Trade, under Liam Fox. After several months, neither was making great progress. DExEU's senior official later wrote that 'it falls to the civil service to be the first line of restraint on an overmighty executive'[21] – a role at which it was all too effective. The EU was insisting on its own proposals for a post-Brexit agreement, and there were no effective counter-proposals from London. The pro-Remain chancellor, Philip Hammond, was accused by colleagues of blocking preparations for a possible 'no deal'. May and her close advisers, principally the former Treasury official Oliver Robbins, were conducting parallel negotiations, apparently without David Davis's knowledge. She wanted a 'bespoke' arrangement with the EU, including a range of special provisions for close future relations, although the experienced (and strongly anti-Brexit) diplomat Sir Ivan Rogers advised that if she was serious about Brexit, she should go for a plain free trade agreement.[22]

One can hardly condemn the EU and its French chief negotiator, Michel Barnier, for proving tough adversaries. The EU's predicament was clear, and hardly concealed. Brexit was a grave setback, and, if possible, it had to be stopped and the referendum nullified, as had happened elsewhere. To deter other possible exits, the UK must be shown not to benefit: 'a country outside the EU cannot have a better deal than an EU member state.'[23] EU officials were sceptical that the UK would actually leave. The attempts by Remain campaigners to prove them right by overturning the referendum meant that the EU had every incentive to be intransigent, which in turn enabled Remainers to assert that Brexit was a disaster.

To capitalize on her early popularity as a 'safe pair of hands', and the Labour leader Jeremy Corbyn's unpopularity, May called a surprise general election for 8 June 2017, in which she was generally expected to triumph. But Labour astutely declared in its manifesto that it accepted the result of the referendum, so Brexit was no longer an issue. It campaigned on more popular ground: opposing austerity. This, combined with May's wooden performance in the campaign, gave Labour sufficient gains to deprive the Conservatives of their seventeen-seat majority, leaving them dependent on the support of the Democratic Unionist Party from Northern Ireland, which held ten seats. Although the Conservatives and Labour, having expressly accepted Brexit, jointly won 82 per cent of the vote, the election result, by weakening the government, reignited the whole Brexit issue both in Parliament and in the country.

Continuing uncertainty about Brexit – what it meant and whether it would happen – galvanized civil society to an extent and with a violence of language and emotion unusual in British (certainly in English) politics. Much of the activity on both sides was spontaneous and small scale, though both also had committed backers willing to spend considerable sums, and both sides alleged foreign interference. Open Britain had begun by campaigning for the rights of EU citizens and to remain in the Single Market. After the 2017 election, it launched a 'People's Vote' campaign for a second referendum, backed by prominent politicians or former politicians and celebrities mainly of the Blairite tendency. During 2018 and 2019 it organized a series of large demonstrations in London. Best for Britain, set up by Gina Miller and various business figures, seems to have raised a large amount of money and subsidized other pro-Remain organizations campaigning for a second referendum. The leading groups shared a common headquarters and a sizeable professional staff. Substantial donations came from the Hungarian-American investor

George Soros (who thought stopping Brexit would be 'good for Britain but would also render Europe a great service by . . . not creating a hard-to-fill hole in the European budget'[24]) and, it was rumoured, Tony Blair. But in 2019 Best for Britain had to appeal discreetly for more money from British and foreign business to finance its grass-roots campaigning.[25] Pro-Brexit groups were slower to organize – they had thought the issue had been decided – operated with less money, and relied more on amateur activity. Several Leave organizers and supporters were investigated by the Electoral Commission in a way they claimed showed bias, and which eventually proved legally groundless. The Commission seems to have been manipulated by Remainer MPs and activists trying to undermine the referendum result.[26] Only when the Brexit Party became active in 2019 was there an organization that dwarfed every other group on both sides.

Business lobbies, EU-funded think-tanks and large corporations played a prominent part on the Remain side, both by putting pressure on politicians and by being used by politicians. Most prominent was the Confederation of British Industry, which is reticent about its small number of full members, dominated by pro-EU multinationals, and including 'industries' such as the BBC and some universities. EU regulation and protectionism suited big corporations. The well-being of British society or British democracy was not their responsibility. Several – including Nissan and Airbus – threatened to move their operations outside the UK in the event of Brexit, only to reverse their positions and pledge greater investment in Britain once Brexit was effectively decided. Boris Johnson's angry comment 'F— business!'[27] no doubt had these lobbies and these attitudes in mind. Many smaller businesses, and most of those who exported outside the EU, were in favour of Leave, but they were little heard or represented.

The EU Commission published its draft Withdrawal Agreement in February 2018, which the former Lib Dem leader Nick Clegg termed a 'humiliation' for Britain, and he endorsed the judgement of a senior French official: 'Do they realise how weak they will be? . . . No self-respecting French politician would put their country in that situation.'[28] At a meeting convened at Chequers on 6 July, a draft White Paper was handed to the Cabinet outlining May's hoped-for 'bespoke' relationship with the EU ('broader in scope than any other that exists between the EU and a third country'). It included staying in the Single Market for trade in goods, agreeing to follow EU rules, and trying to avoid possible problems at the Irish border by effectively remaining in the EU Customs Union (by a complex 'Facilitated Customs Agreement'); but free immigration from the EU would be restrained. Any minister who did not accept it, the press were told, could resign and, without their ministerial cars, get taxis home. David Davis left his resignation till two days later, as did Foreign Secretary Boris Johnson and the Europe minister, Steve Baker. The EU subsequently rejected the White Paper: there could be no 'cherry picking' of the Single Market's free movement of people, goods, services and capital, and no special customs arrangement. The EU thus rejected the best offer it was ever to get.

The Chequers meeting brought into prominence a division between 'Leavers' and 'Remainers' in the Conservative Party, and particularly among its MPs, of whom some 185 supported Remain and 144 Leave. They represented different views of what the party represented. One was that it was essentially managerial, and the party of business. Its purpose, bluntly, was to make everyone (or at least its voters) richer. The other view was more traditionally 'Tory': the party represented the nation, its unity and its traditions. The former view predominantly supported Remain, the big-business consensus, and included many leading figures – 'grandees' such as Sir John Major, Kenneth Clarke and Lord Heseltine, ministers, former ministers, would-be ministers.

The Labour Party too was divided. Jeremy Corbyn represented the old Labour Left, which had always been hostile to the EU as a capitalist club whose laws and regulations were a barrier to socialism: his beliefs helped to hold the party back from fully supporting Remain. But most Labour MPs and party members were Remainers, sometimes instinctively and passionately so, showing how far the Labour Party had become 'a city-centric party of middle-class public-sector workers and their teenagers'.[29] Around a third of Labour supporters in the country were strongly for Leave, however, particularly working-class Midlanders and Northerners. Approximately 161 Labour-held constituencies had voted Leave, and only 70 had voted Remain. This would be decisive in the 2019 general election.[30]

Following the rejection of the Chequers White Paper, a new draft agreement was published on 14 November 2018 by the May government and the EU. The latest DExEU secretary, Dominic Raab, immediately resigned – the second incumbent to do so – on the grounds that 'no democratic nation has ever signed up to . . . such an extensive regime without any democratic control.' In other circumstances, this agreement might have become the definitive form of Brexit – or 'Brexit in name only' (BRINO), as critics dubbed it. It consisted of a

Withdrawal Agreement having the force of international law, and a Political Declaration, said (rather disingenuously) not to be legally binding, which set out the principles of the future relationship between the UK and the EU.

Michael Gove remained as the principal Brexiteer in the Cabinet, seemingly believing that this agreement was the only alternative to no Brexit at all. Some who took this view, including several leading backbench Brexiteers, believed that the UK could sign up to a disadvantageous 'deal' and renounce it later. A small group of Conservative MPs – sometimes called the Spartans, the diehard element of the loose Conservative 'European Research Group'[31] – thought this too great a risk. But they themselves were obliged to take an equal risk: if May's new agreement were defeated in the Commons, Remainers might manage to stop Brexit altogether. With hindsight, had Remainers backed May's deal, it would have resulted in BRINO, probably split the Conservative Party, and perhaps put Corbyn into Downing Street. But they chose instead to campaign for a second referendum.

This Withdrawal Agreement would have placed the UK in a position without parallel in modern international relations. It would have kept Britain for an indefinite transitional period under the authority of EU law, including legislation passed after it had left the EU, and under the ultimate jurisdiction of the European Court of Justice. Some saw an analogy with the 'unequal treaties' imposed by the imperialist powers on nineteenth-century China. Neutral arbitration was explicitly excluded, although it is 'virtually unheard of in international treaty relations for states to agree to be bound by decisions of tribunals which are not strictly neutral'.[32] Examples of practical disadvantages included subordination to

EU economic decisions, over which Britain would have had no control, in competition, trade, social, agricultural, fishing, environmental, state-aid and tax policies.

The crucial feature of the Agreement was the 'Irish backstop'. Ireland's relationships with the EU and the UK are delicate. Increased dependency on Brussels is the price of reduced dependency on London. Brexit calls this equilibrium into question given Ireland's economic links with the UK, its main trading partner. It also creates political problems. For moderate Irish nationalists, common EU citizenship in the Republic and Northern Ireland had glossed over the emotive problem of the border: it could be imagined in effect no longer to exist. Brexit meant that an economic border would exist once again. Some worried that 'the Troubles' might even be reignited — or at least saw political advantage in evoking this danger. They included the EU, which now claimed to be a guarantor of peace. The DUP, on whom Theresa May's parliamentary majority relied, opposed anything that separated Northern Ireland and Great Britain. At first, the problem seemed a practical one: there should be no 'hard border' with customs posts and barriers. From Britain came a series of suggestions — eventually very detailed ones[33] — to avoid a hard border through prior customs declarations, electronic tracking and 'trusted trader' schemes. They were dismissed by Brussels and Dublin as 'magical thinking', even though one of the schemes was founded on a report originally commissioned by the European Parliament.[34]

Whether it would have been more sensible for Dublin to try to resolve the border question rather than aggravating it by 'excessive europhile zeal and with a touch of old-fashioned Anglophobia'[35] only time will tell. It is unclear whether Brussels was supporting Dublin (whose politicians were competing to prove their national credentials), or Dublin was obeying Brussels (where the border provided an invaluable lever). Ireland had endured Greek-style austerity under a compulsory EU 'bailout' in 2010, creating high youth unemployment and a stagnant economy. This had been 'swept under the carpet'[36] as Irish and EU politicians claimed that austerity had restored economic growth. This was a façade, however, as Ireland's GDP figures were swollen by vast funds channelled through the country by multinationals: it was in effect a huge tax haven, which enabled its nominal GDP to increase by 26 per cent in 2015.[37] Though this greatly benefited a minority, overall Irish living standards were 10–20 per cent lower than in the North (which, incidentally, makes unification impractical).[38] The tax-haven status depended on EU forbearance, which was wearing thin. It seems likely that Ireland had no real choice but to follow the Brussels line of intransigence over the border issue, but it played to Irish nationalism too.

The EU refused to discuss future trading relations (on which the border issue logically depended) and instead demanded, and the British government accepted, that an 'Irish backstop' should be agreed to prevent a 'hard border' and supposedly to safeguard the Good Friday peace agreement. The backstop would require Northern Ireland to remain in the EU Customs Union and Single Market (effectively as 'a colony of the European Union . . . legally semi-detached from the rest of this country'[39]), and dependent on Dublin to protect its interests in Brussels, thus undermining the Union and even the peace. Alternatively, the whole United Kingdom would have in effect to suspend Brexit until the EU unilaterally decided that the border issue had been satisfactorily resolved.

Theresa May's fateful choice was that the whole UK should remain in the Customs Union and close to the Single Market, subject to EU law and regulation for as long as the EU saw fit. This evidently placed the UK in a position of hopeless inferiority in future negotiations, and risked 'dropping the UK into a legal black hole'.[40] For all these reasons, the Agreement was too much for Parliament. The Spartans saw it as nullifying Brexit: worse than full EU membership, and worse than a 'no-deal' exit. Remainers agreed that full EU membership was better and hoped that opposing the government might lead to stalemate and a second referendum.

The difficulty of the government's position was patent. It had passed the European Union (Withdrawal) Act in 2018, but with an amendment to require it, if it could not reach an agreement with the EU, or if Parliament rejected the agreement, to come forward with further proposals for the House of Commons to debate and hold 'a meaningful vote' on. However, this Act also required another Act of Parliament to implement any agreement with the EU. This meant that, without such an Act, the UK would automatically leave the EU when the two-year negotiation period under Article 50 of the Treaty of Lisbon came to an end on 29 March 2019. This confused and contradictory situation reflected the disagreements in the House of Commons. The loss of its majority, and divisions within the Conservative Party, meant that the government could not force any policy through.

When its Withdrawal Agreement was presented to the Commons for a 'meaningful vote' on 15 January 2019, it was defeated by 432 votes to 202 – the biggest ever parliamentary defeat of any government. May agreed to give Parliament a vote on whether to rule out a 'no deal', that is, to rule out leaving the EU without a Withdrawal Agreement. After some modification to try to reduce the risks created by the 'backstop', the Agreement was presented again to the Commons on 12 March, and, more narrowly but still decisively, was defeated by 391 votes to 242. The next day, the Commons voted to instruct the government to seek an extension to EU membership while negotiations continued.[41]

The traditional remedy for such a situation would have been for a government to resign and ask the Queen to dissolve Parliament. But the Cameron–Clegg coalition government had passed the Fixed-term Parliaments Act (2011), which abolished the royal prerogative of dissolution and allowed an early general election only if at least two-thirds of the Commons agreed. So, with astonishing fortitude or bovine stubbornness, depending on one's sympathies, the prime minister battled on, making a string of concessions to the Opposition and Remainers.

The government was now to face a constitutional challenge unprecedented in the democratic era. Several months before, in December 2018, the speaker of the House of Commons, John Bercow, had allowed the Conservative Remainer and former attorney general Dominic Grieve to move amendments that openly broke parliamentary conventions and overturned decisions previously made – a sign of things to come. On 22 March 2019 (a week before the UK was due formally to leave the EU), the government applied for a short extension of membership to 12 April, hoping that MPs would in the end support its Withdrawal Agreement rather than permit a no-deal exit. On 27 March, the speaker allowed MPs to seize the agenda to hold 'indicative votes' on alternative policies, but farcically all eight proposals were rejected. On the 29th, the government put forward the Withdrawal Agreement alone (for the third time), without the Political Declaration, but this too was voted down, by 344 to 286. On 3 April, the speaker again allowed parliamentary rules to be suspended to introduce the 'Cooper–Letwin Bill'[42] to force a further extension of EU membership to 31 October, thus removing the government's ability to put pressure on MPs. It was evident that this would not be the last attempt by a cross-party Remainer majority in the Commons to dictate government policy and force repeated extensions of EU membership. The reason, or pretext, was to prevent the UK from leaving the EU without a Withdrawal Agreement – or 'crashing out' and going over the 'cliff edge', as Remainers habitually put it, spiced with predictions of chaos at the ports and economic disaster. The hope was that repeated delays would eventually lead to a second referendum. The prime minister even hinted at this on 21 May 2019 – anathema to Leavers in her party. It seemed possible that the whole party system might be reshaped, as had happened in the 1840s, 1880s and 1920s, with the old parties (especially the Conservatives) splitting and new anti- and pro-Brexit parties forming.

European elections had reluctantly to be held on 23 May 2019 as Britain had extended its membership of the EU. European and Irish citizens in the UK could also vote. This became a quasi-referendum on Brexit, and it showed a thoroughly divided and polarized country. A brand-new Brexit Party (a supercharged UKIP, now attracting wider cross-party support, and being less a vehicle for Nigel Farage) won 30 per cent of the votes and 40 per cent of seats, becoming the largest party in the European Parliament. The Liberal Democrats, outright Remainers, were second, topping the poll in

London. Labour (which had maintained a studied ambiguousness) came third. The Conservatives achieved their worst ever showing in a national poll. With a derisory 8.8 per cent of the vote, they lost fifteen of their nineteen seats: a stunning warning that they faced annihilation if they did not take a stronger Brexit line, but might recover if they did. Even before the vote took place, Theresa May had finally given up the struggle and announced that she would resign.

After a contest between supporters and opponents of the May 'deal', the Conservative Party elected Boris Johnson – who had resigned from the Cabinet after the Chequers 'ambush' – as leader, and he became prime minister on 24 July. Johnson was widely distrusted within his own party and beyond, and detested by Remainers, who subjected him to an unusual level of personal abuse and sought ways of bringing him down. But his election as leader showed that the Conservative Party was now an unambiguously Brexit party. He promptly carried out the biggest Cabinet purge since the Second World War.[43]

Speaker Bercow and leading Remainer MPs, most prominently Sir Oliver Letwin, Dominic Grieve and Hilary Benn, led new attempts to seize control of government policy in a way not seen since the English Civil War – tragedy repeating itself as farce. They again seized the agenda of the Commons to impose actions on the government, contravening constitutional principles central to parliamentary government for two centuries. In response, some lawyers urged the government to prorogue (i.e. suspend) Parliament – a power it explicitly possessed under the Fixed-term Parliaments Act. To forestall this possibility MPs passed legislation, by dubiously constitutional means, to force the government to recall

Parliament at set intervals. Gina Miller and the former Conservative prime minister John Major threatened to bring legal
proceedings against the Johnson government to prevent any
such prorogation.

This was an incipient constitutional crisis, even though,
looking back, its absurdities perhaps outweigh its dramas.
Ever since the referendum, some Remainers had been arguing that 'parliamentary sovereignty' meant that the House of
Commons was the supreme authority in the country. In fact,
parliamentary sovereignty was confined to legislation: 'the
right to make or unmake any law . . . neither more nor less'.[44]
Moreover, the legal sovereign was 'the Crown in Parliament',
implying the co-operation and consent of both, 'functioning together as a law-making body'.[45] This co-ordination of
executive and legislative powers is a defining feature of British parliamentary government. Parliament does not possess
executive power, which some now wanted it to seize. There
were even wild rumours that it might set up a governing
committee — real shades of the seventeenth century. In no
modern state does the legislature have such authority; in all
democratic systems, the executive necessarily has its own
powers and responsibilities, for which it answers not only to
parliament, but also to the electorate. But some MPs seemed
set on a quasi-oligarchy, based on a misunderstood and now
archaic idea of parliamentary sovereignty which was 'flatly
inconsistent with established constitutional principles'.[46] MPs
repeatedly refused to vote no confidence in the government —
their constitutional right and duty if they opposed its
policy — because this would almost certainly lead to a general
election. Instead, with the assistance of the speaker and the
Supreme Court, they forced the government to act against its

own policy, creating brief episodes of unconstitutional, irresponsible and hence undemocratic government.

Underlying questions of constitutional propriety was the fundamental issue: could Parliament legitimately overrule a referendum which it had itself legislated for, despite formal promises that the result would be honoured? Diehard Remainers said yes, but cooler heads sought roundabout methods. The government was hamstrung by the Fixed-term Parliaments Act, so a hostile majority could trap Johnson in office but without power. Remainers inside and outside Parliament intended to force the government (as the catchphrase went) 'to take "no deal" off the table', so that until a deal was reached the government would be required by legislation to request indefinite extensions to Britain's membership of the EU under Article 50 of the Lisbon Treaty. This would make it impossible to negotiate equitably with Brussels – as Johnson colourfully put it, it would 'chop the legs out from under the UK' – as the government would be unable to refuse the EU's terms. Either it would be forced to agree to a 'soft Brexit' as an appendage of the EU, or the stalemate would be prolonged indefinitely. Remainers hoped that the public, disillusioned and impatient, would acquiesce in a second referendum ('People's Vote') to reverse the first vote. This, unlike the first referendum, they proclaimed, would be binding. If the vote went their way, the UK would remain in the EU, or, if it had already left, plead to be readmitted on terms unknown. The international humiliation and domestic outrage this would cause seemed not to trouble its proponents.

Boris Johnson repeatedly promised not to request another extension of EU membership – he said on 5 September he would rather be 'dead in a ditch'. The House of Commons, returning from its summer recess, again seized control of business, and with the support of some twenty Remainer Conservative MPs, including former ministers, passed the 'Benn Act',[47] which became law on 9 September. Principally, it dictated a letter that Johnson was required to send to the EU requesting an extension. Enthusiasts menaced him with impeachment and being 'sent to prison' if he disobeyed.[48] The Act was unconstitutional, as it summarily infringed the royal prerogative by attempting to dictate foreign policy, but the government did not force a crisis which, among other things, might have involved the monarch refusing consent to major legislation for the first time for three centuries.

The prime minister had already advised the Queen on 28 August to prorogue parliament from mid-September to mid-October, a longer period than usual, with the clear if unstated intention of limiting further infringement of executive powers. In September, Scottish nationalists and Gina Miller asked the Scottish and English courts for a judgment that the prorogation was unlawful. The Scottish Court of Session and the English High Court of Justice (the lord chief justice, the master of the rolls, and the president of the Queen's Bench sitting as a Divisional Court) both at first dismissed the case. The action, the English judges said, was an attempt 'to invite the judicial arm of the state to exercise hitherto unidentified power over the Executive branch of the state in its dealings with Parliament'. Their conclusion was that the government had acted within its long-established powers in a matter of political judgement, hence 'the decision of the Prime Minister to advise Her Majesty the Queen to prorogue Parliament is not justiciable in Her Majesty's courts.'[49] The case then went to the Supreme

Court, which on 24 September ignored the earlier judgment and declared the prorogation 'unlawful, null and of no effect'. It thus overturned more than 300 years of constitutional practice, and broke Article 9 of the Bill of Rights (1689), which prohibits 'any court' from questioning 'proceedings in parliament'. One eminent legal scholar described the judgment as 'wholly unjustified by law', 'a misuse of judicial power', and 'radically destabilizing' of government.[50] This turned out not to matter quite as much as it seemed; soon afterwards the electorate reasserted its authority in a general election in which it could see clearly what was at stake, and what the various parties stood for.

And yet these constitutional tussles mattered for what they made visible. The members of the Supreme Court, following the EU's mode of jurisprudence, had made a judgment that was 'neither legal nor constitutional, but purely political'. It 'would unhesitatingly have been rejected by all previous generations of judges back to the Bill of Rights'.[51] A majority of MPs and their speaker – whose unchecked powers were entrusted to him on the presumption of his complete integrity – had taken or tried to take blatantly unconstitutional actions. Many civil servants had pushed their own political line, sometimes with the connivance of Remainer ministers, sometimes behind their backs. Some even privately warned ministers that they might refuse to obey instructions.[52]

Of course, they could argue – and did argue – that the electorate was uncertain, or poorly informed, or had changed its mind. These arguments would undermine every democracy based on the rule of law: any election result could be said to be based on misunderstanding; any majority could be said to have changed if some opinion poll suggested it. At times during 2019, it seemed that the UK was barely a functioning democracy. As had happened elsewhere in Europe, a powerful section of the elite put membership of the EU above all other considerations or duties. Whether for reasons of ideology, professional interest, or fear, they had attempted by outright opposition, delay and subterfuge to substitute their own preferences, however sincerely held they might have been, for those of the electorate. They were trying to impose limits on democratic choice, as had been done most recently in Italy and Greece. This issue was far more fundamental than the uncertain economic gains or losses of leaving or remaining. It inflamed divisions in the country and threatened to cause a collapse in public trust in the whole political and legal system with consequences none could foresee.

The political class drew back gradually from the brink. The victory of the Brexit Party in the European elections had been a warning. On 17 October, a compromise Withdrawal Agreement was concluded by the EU and the UK, with the agreement of the leading Brexiteers. On the 21st, the EU (Withdrawal Agreement) Bill was introduced by the government, but its passage was delayed by MPs determined to force another extension to EU membership. Downing Street duly sent the letter prescribed by the Benn Act, unceremoniously delivered without the prime minister's signature, requesting an extension until 31 January 2020. Britain was made to look ridiculous and ungovernable, but this was evidently considered a price worth paying to humiliate Johnson and damage his popularity. In fact, it played into his hands by painting his opponents as recklessly irresponsible. The insistence of the House of Commons on keeping a government in office without the means to determine the most pressing national question was increasingly indefensible. Opposition parties found it more and more difficult to refuse a general election. The Remain group Open Britain broke up acrimoniously.[53] Even so, it was only when the Liberal Democrats and the Scottish National Party thought an election might bring them gains that they broke ranks with Labour and supported an election through a special Act of Parliament. An abortive attempt was made to affect the result by giving the vote to sixteen- and seventeen-year olds and to EU nationals by a simple amendment – yet another unconstitutional ploy, prevented by the deputy speaker. On 6 November Parliament was at last dissolved, and a general election took place on 12 December.

Unlike the 2017 election, this one was principally, if not wholly, about Brexit. Labour was divided, though it managed to agree – Corbyn unenthusiastically – on offering a second referendum. The Liberal Democrats brazenly promised to override the 2016 referendum and remain in the EU. The Conservatives were now, for the first time, united: Remainer MPs, however senior, who had supported the attacks on the government were ejected from the parliamentary party; some were deselected by their own constituencies; some joined other parties or founded their own – the path to political oblivion. The Brexit Party agreed not to stand against sitting Conservatives.

The election, as predicted, was decided in the Leave-voting Labour constituencies of the Midlands and North: in England and Wales, 80 per cent of Labour's most vulnerable seats (where the Conservatives were in second place) had voted Leave in 2016.[54] Despite three years of passionate debate, the choice voters had expressed in 2016 still stood: most people, it seems, were determined not to be badgered into changing their minds. But the Remain vote was divided, especially between Labour and the Lib Dems, and Labour had its worst result since 1935. Boris Johnson proved an effective campaigner, promising simply to 'Get Brexit done'. This slogan (like 'Take back control' in the referendum) was credited to the saturnine Dominic Cummings, his *éminence grise*. The loathing felt for Johnson by many left-wing activists was evidently not shared by working-class voters, and the Conservatives won twenty-four previously solid Labour seats, the so-called 'Red Wall', some of which had never voted Tory before. As the journalist Janice Turner put it, 'in much of the north [whether] Leave or Remain, the majority belief is that a binding referendum result should be honoured. We should celebrate that in these chaotic times, our fellow citizens uphold the rule of law.'[55] The electoral system did what it was meant to do: it delivered a parliamentary majority based on the largest coherent body of opinion.

The Conservatives gained forty-seven seats in all, giving the party a majority of eighty. They might well have won another thirty if the Brexit Party had not stood in winnable Labour constituencies. This was the sixth general election in a row in which the Conservatives had increased their share of the vote, which at 43.6 per cent was the highest won by any party for forty years. Only in Scotland were they beaten – by the SNP, which won 45 per cent of the vote. The Conservatives were the most popular party with every age group over thirty-nine, and they led in every single socio-economic category, most of all among C2s (less-skilled workers). The Conservative Party was now more working class, and the Labour Party more middle class, than ever. It may be that this will be seen as a historic election, in which a realignment of loyalties, which had been building for some time, finally took place.[56]

Johnson was now leading a solidly pro-Brexit government with a large majority. But its options were constrained by May's Withdrawal Agreement, to which the EU understandably clung, and which Johnson felt obliged to accept with only limited changes. He managed to revise the Northern Ireland Protocol, adding an 'escape clause' that required a vote in Northern Ireland to continue the arrangement after four years – though clearly 'escape' was not guaranteed. The Political Declaration was made less constraining and more conducive to a free trade agreement without EU control of future British policy. In the meantime, Northern Ireland remained de facto in the EU Customs Union and much of its Single Market, unless and until a future free trade agreement with the EU solved the problem by removing the need for border checks anywhere. There would thus be an economic border between Northern Ireland and Great Britain, which gave significant leverage to the EU even if the UK government sought to make customs checks as light as possible. The Withdrawal Agreement contained other perilous small print. There was open-ended acceptance of ultimate European Court jurisdiction in some disputes (rejected by Norway and Switzerland, for example); and also vaguely worded agreements to unspecified financial obligations (far beyond the 'divorce bill'), also to be interpreted by the European Court – a situation wholly outside the normal practice of international law, which is neutral arbitration. Brexiteers accepted this as the best outcome available.[57] But the benefits for Britain in this Agreement are very hard to find. The responsibility lies essentially with the May government and the 2017 Parliament.

The modified Withdrawal Agreement Bill was passed by the new Parliament on 20 December, and the Agreement was signed on the 24th by Ursula von der Leyen, the new president of the European Commission, Charles Michel, president of the European Council, and Boris Johnson. Britain duly left the EU at 11 p.m. (midnight in Brussels) on 31 January 2020, 1,317 days since the referendum. Brexiteers celebrated as much in relief as in triumph.

Many Leavers had found Remainer machinations uncomfortably close to treachery, and some said so. Nevertheless, the constitution, though strained, had finally worked, and flagrant weak points (most obviously the Fixed-term Parliaments Act) had been highlighted. Tempers and language had been inflamed, but there had been little or no violence, and demonstrations had been noisy but generally good humoured. We were fortunate: in France, during the first three months of the *gilets jaunes* protests against EU-inspired austerity in 2018, 11 people died and around 3,000 were injured.[58] Yet our turmoil had been held up as a dreadful example to the whole of Europe and had thereby strengthened the EU; it was difficult to imagine other member countries following in Britain's footsteps except in extreme crisis and probably with a breakdown of law and order. Perhaps it was only in Britain that there *could* be a 'democratic choice against the European treaties', and that 'powerful backroom interests' did *not* have the final say.

6. COVID and After

'People make their own history, but not freely: they
cannot choose the circumstances.'

Karl Marx, 1852[1]

A new coronavirus from China – 'COVID-19' – made its
presence felt in Europe in February 2020. The first major
impact was in northern Italy, perhaps because many Chinese workers were employed in Chinese-owned luxury goods
factories there. It spread, mainly through tourism, to Spain,
Germany, France, Britain and beyond. At first it seemed a
mild disease, no worse than seasonal flu, but in a few weeks
it turned the world upside down. Many compared the sudden
crisis with war, and there were some parallels: the disruption
of ordinary life, the huge increase in state controls, the cat-
astrophic interruption of economic activity, the consequent
transformation of public finances, even the number of deaths
and long-term collateral damage to health and welfare. It also
created, like wars, an early sense of unity, which, again as in
wars, began to fray under the stresses created. Like war it will
probably bring about geopolitical and ideological shifts. And
it imposed a test on societies – their solidarity, their efficiency,
and their resilience. Whether Britain would ride out the storm
better outside the EU would be seen as the first test of Brexit.
Whether the Eurozone could cope with new financial stresses
would be the latest ordeal for the EU: it was, Angela Merkel

told the European Parliament, 'the greatest test the European Union has ever faced'.

Various parts of the planet were affected very differently, for a combination of reasons that are still not wholly apparent: average age, population density, urbanization, levels of internal and international mobility, obesity, ethnicity, poverty, effectiveness of public health systems, climate, and actions of governments. Every country and system responded in ways that seemed bizarre confirmations of national stereotypes. Americans bought more guns. Sweden relied on individual good sense. Germans showed remarkable discipline. In Spain and France forms had to be filled in to leave the house, large forces of police were mobilized and hundreds of thousands of fines levied. In Britain – where the Queen made two remarkable addresses to the nation – most people clearly wanted to 'do their bit' and 'save the NHS' by doing as they were told with little complaint or compulsion.

The bad-tempered Brexit arguments seemed forgotten. We joined neighbourhood groups, clapped the NHS, smiled at strangers as we gave them a wide berth, and invented new and ingenious ways of keeping in touch. As the Queen movingly put it on 8 May, 'our streets are not empty; they are filled with the love and the care that we have for each other.' More people than were ever needed volunteered to help the NHS or their neighbours. Centenarian 'Captain Tom' Moore and child amputee Tony Hudgell touched many hearts as they walked to raise money for hospitals. Some people grumbled about interferences with their liberties, and others about the government's failure to give strict-enough instructions. Many got extremely annoyed about Dominic Cummings's jaunt to Barnard Castle. It seemed that another cultural division was emerging, with intriguing similarities with the Brexit divide: conformists versus libertarians, the worried against the confident.[2]

Countries close to China, and wary of it, had reacted fast and effectively, including South Korea, New Zealand, Australia and Singapore (which had a special hospital standing empty and ready, together with the testing capacity to track and quarantine those infected). Some that had prepared for a long-expected epidemic – including the USA and Britain, which had been classed by the Global Health Security Index as the two best – proved unprepared for this new virus. The lavishly funded, decentralized and mostly private health system in Germany coped well; but that in America coped badly. Britain arguably suffered from 'a longstanding fixation with centralized control'[3] shared by officials and politicians, and indeed by much of the public. Public Health England (the agency responsible for health planning) and the NHS – whose hospital staff set a high example of professional devotion – seem to have been cautious and slow to respond to the unexpected. Ventilators were rapidly produced, but simpler and as it turned out more useful equipment (protective clothing and masks) remained in short supply, largely because stocks had been run down and the plan for replacement relied on imports from countries which kept deliveries for themselves. The NHS proved able to improvise big new hospitals, but they turned out not to be needed. It also decided to clear the hospitals for an expected influx of seriously ill patients, but this helped to spread COVID to old people's homes, where the major disaster took place. In August, the government decided to abolish Public Health England and set up a new pandemic defence agency. Devolved governments – especially the Scottish – claimed to be dealing with the pandemic better than the UK government.

Ministers seemed to be at the mercy of the health system (over which they had limited direct control), of changing and sometimes erratic scientific advice, and of modelling based on earlier influenza epidemics. Boris Johnson and others in government themselves became ill in April, Johnson seriously: both a symbol and a real sign of faltering leadership. Government policy at first seemed to be to allow the disease to spread and create natural immunity. Then it turned to 'lockdown': less strictly than in draconian New Zealand but more so than in libertarian Sweden. It is unclear whether drastic lockdown measures made the crucial difference, how and when they should be ended, or how much damage they ultimately cause. Were hand-washing and other sensible precautions the key? Or should the government have been stricter sooner?

As the weeks passed, the government was satisfying neither the libertarians nor the lockdown enthusiasts. It gave the impression of being buffeted by unexpected events. It was certainly buffeted by its many enemies, who developed remarkable powers of hindsight. Incessant, often sensational, and predominantly critical media coverage created a ceaseless political challenge. The coverage gave a more than usually insular view of the crisis; apart from opaque statistics and an obsession with holiday prospects, it was difficult to get any real sense of how other countries were managing, and hence impossible to judge the British government other than superficially. Nevertheless, in both policy and performance, it appeared mediocre. Damningly, Britain appeared by the summer to have suffered higher mortality than almost any other country; but the statistics were not always comparable, nor of course did they take account of very different national conditions. In most European countries except Sweden, governments took very similar measures and met very similar problems.

A final verdict is not possible at the time of writing, especially as many countries that previously seemed to have beaten the epidemic started in late summer to see sharp increases in cases, putting several in a worse position than the UK. Behind the headlines, there were improvements: by August, supply problems were solved, Britain developed Europe's biggest testing capacity, and cases and hospitalization rates fell steeply. How well the UK could weather a likely 'second wave' of the disease which loomed in the autumn and winter would show whether the government was capable of learning from earlier failings and redeeming itself with the public.

As early as May and June came a reminder of how the socio-economic damage already caused by the pandemic – most obviously unemployment and the suspension of schools and universities – could inflame existing tensions. There were sporadic riots in Germany, Italy, Spain, France, the USA and Israel protesting against aspects of the lockdown. Most shockingly, the killing of a black man, George Floyd, by police in America on 25 May, which was videoed and shown universally, led to an explosion of anger and violence in the worst civil unrest since the 1960s. Similar protests were actively instigated in Europe. On 2 June there was a violent demonstration in Paris, at which rubber bullets were fired, and riots in several other cities. There were demonstrations in Germany, the Netherlands, Italy and Switzerland. In Bristol, on 7 June the statue of a local worthy involved in the seventeenth-century slave trade was pulled down. A protest in Westminster saw the police attacked and the statue of Churchill vandalized with the inscription 'Racist'.

This ballooned into a campaign to 'topple the racists', a multi-ethnic student-led attack on a range of public symbols and figures said to have a connection – sometimes tenuous to the point of invisibility – with slavery or imperialism. One sceptical observer suggested that 'people will shrug their shoulders at the weariness of this overwrought generation of Britons who, having locked themselves up for more than two months, emerged to fight statues and ghosts.'[4] The campaign had no ostensible connection with Brexit, but there was evidently a considerable overlap as students staged another rebellion against the national identity of their elders and their social inferiors. The attack on symbols aimed not to 'erase history', as some suggested, but to define what version of history should be made official, and who its beneficiaries should be. Targets included even Gladstone and Peel, the progressive heroes of their day, showing that every part of the national past was potentially under attack. This was encouraged by many in positions of authority in universities, museums and even the civil service. If Brexit had been for some a culture war, a second bout was beginning.

The global economy had collapsed faster under the pandemic's restrictions even than in 1929, with precipitous falls in output and rises in unemployment. From the beginning, the hope had been that until a cure had been found or the pandemic had retreated, governments could place economies in 'suspended animation' ready for recovery, supporting employment and consumption by borrowing and spending.[5] Governments consequently accumulated debt at a rate unimaginable since the Second World War. The potential catastrophe was greater still in developing countries with weaker health systems and less financial resilience.

The COVID crisis tested systems at their weakest points, which for the EU was financial fragility. As noted in Chapter 3, the Eurozone was already unstable. After years of slow and uneven growth, it was marked by wide divergences in living standards and unemployment, trade imbalances, and dangerously high and unequal levels of state and private debt which threatened the banking system and hence the whole economy. By 2020, several EU member states were among the most indebted in the developed world, including Greece (public debt 180% of annual GDP), Italy (154%), Portugal (136%), Belgium (124%), France (116%), and Spain (115%).[6] UK growth was higher, and its debt lower (85% of GDP).

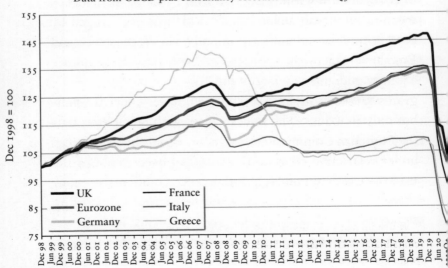

Real GDP growth: UK and Eurozone, 1998–2021
Data from OECD plus consultancy forecasts from 2020 Q3 to 2021 Q2

The COVID crisis hit several of these indebted states hardest: Italy, Belgium, Spain, and France. It required their governments to spend and borrow vastly more, while depressing their revenues. It devastated tourism, on which southern Europe greatly depended. Frightening levels of bankruptcy and unemployment loomed. Even more than the previous Eurozone crisis, the pandemic demanded an unprecedented level of mutual aid, including a huge transfer of resources from the northern to the southern member states.

The EU states' first reactions to the epidemic showed dismaying limits to solidarity. Exports of medical equipment were embargoed, and frontiers were closed. Nicole Gnesotto, vice-president of the Jacques Delors Institute, lamented in April that 'the EU's lack of preparations, its powerlessness, its timidity are staggering.'[7] Angela Merkel told the European Parliament in July that 'Eurosceptics are waiting to misuse the crisis for their own ends. We must show them the added value of co-operation within the European Union', but she added meaningfully that such co-operation 'must not excessively burden only the economically strong member states'. She and Emmanuel Macron had proposed a rescue package centred on a jointly guaranteed loan of €500 billion, to be distributed as grants to the hard-hit states. An extra €250 billion was added, but only in loans.* The novelty was that, for the first time, the European Commission could borrow money itself, though under restrictive conditions and as a temporary measure. Had the EU again found its customary last-minute solution?

---

* If Britain had still been in the EU, it would have been the second largest contributor to EU budgets, liable during the next budgetary cycle for €84 billion.

Less than was claimed. Support for the southern economies required huge grants to governments and companies to sustain employment and consumption. But an exhausting and bad-tempered meeting of the European Council on 21 July had agreed only half-measures. The total of the grants was reduced to €390 billion.

On both sides, the arguments were all too understandable. The southern states demanded unstinting and unaccountable financial aid from countries that had done very well out of the EU; but the northern states (not only Germany, but also the Netherlands, the Scandinavian countries and Austria) were reluctant to sign blank cheques, especially if that meant subsidizing competitors to their own industries, and donating to countries with higher social spending, more tax evasion, and sometimes less COVID illness than they themselves were experiencing. National stereotypes coloured the argument: a mean and selfish North versus a corrupt and feckless South.

The agreement, despite extravagant hype, satisfied few who understood it. EU governments were individually trying to salvage their stricken economies, but within their varying means. Germany was able to match the UK and USA with close to 9 per cent of GDP in direct grant support for its own economy, but poorer and/or more indebted countries could manage less than half this figure. The EU's rescue effort added only a derisory 0.5 per cent of GDP per annum in grants for four years, starting only in 2021 – too little, too late. The rest of the package was in loans, equal to only about 1 per cent of GDP per annum, and to be made to already over-indebted countries, some of which refused the loans due to their stringent conditions. Moreover, the grants are to be repaid from future EU budgets. Even then, the 'frugal' countries insisted on the right to delay payments and impose conditions, and most also insisted on rebates to themselves. European solidarity again proved thin gruel. By August 2020, the Italian economy had gone back to its levels of the early 1990s. The EU rescue package was to give it €10 billion in 2021, but its budget deficit for 2020 alone was heading for €260 billion. Alarming signs of deflation were also appearing by the autumn of 2020, a potentially disastrous aggravation.[8]

In the meantime, the southern economies were being sustained by the European Central Bank, which was lending hand over fist. In March it began buying €750 billion-worth of mainly Italian, French and Spanish government bonds, a way of subsidizing public spending and private borrowing. This was in addition to €300 billion recently disbursed by the Bank, and brought its total Eurozone bond purchases since 2015 to €2.6 trillion.[9] At the time of writing, the ECB was on the way towards holding nearly half of Italian public debt. Financial experts disagreed as to whether, or for how long, this mountain of debt was sustainable. It certainly depended on political agreement within the EU. But on 5 May the German Constitutional Court had ruled that the purchases might be unlawful, and ordered the German Central Bank to withdraw its participation in three months' time unless evidence was provided that the purchases were 'proportionate'. Moreover, it ruled that the European Court of Justice (ECJ) (which claims sole and supreme jurisdiction over European law) had acted wrongly and beyond its powers: it was, the German court asserted, the member states which were 'guardians of the treaties', not the ECJ. This pulled away the legal prop of the EU's supranational authority. Confrontation was averted, at least for the time being, when documents were quietly disclosed by the ECB to the German government, which declared itself satisfied – a face-saving outcome hardly reported in the media.

This episode gave another indication of the power of Germany to make or break European policies, and of the reluctance of the German state and many German politicians – whatever the views of the present German government – to allow fundamental decisions to be taken by 'Europe' when German taxpayers and savers stand to foot the bill. Germany's enviable financial surpluses enabled it to launch a vastly greater fiscal stimulus package for its own economy than any other EU member, including subsidies to German corporations, which would inevitably increase its dominance of the Eurozone. As Joseph Stiglitz had warned, 'Without a course correction, the euro will become little more than a tool for *German* prosperity.'[10] How long before it sucks the life out of its captive market? The German government is looking beyond Europe, and in August published a report outlining its ambitions in Asia.[11]

The British government, led by its newly appointed chancellor of the exchequer, Rishi Sunak, implemented an effective policy as early as March, combining grants, loans, tax reliefs, support for workers on 'furlough', and income support.[12] This seems to have been a well-judged package, within affordable financial limits: its support schemes would cost around £188 billion, which, when added to lost revenue of some £116 billion, would mean increasing the public deficit for 2020 by over £300 billion, or 15 per cent of GDP. This helped to sustain the economy without risking a credit crisis or later inflation.[13] The United States also undertook huge financial support measures. So did Germany, as we have seen. By July, Britain seemed to have suffered more economic damage than most, however: an accumulated economic loss of 21 per cent of GDP – slightly less than Spain, slightly more than France and Italy, and much worse than Germany. But by the autumn (see graph, p. 132) its economy was recovering faster than most of the world, with manufacturing and financial services in the lead.[14] However painful its job losses, they were the smallest of any major European country, and the government's financial deficit, though huge, was consistently lower than the Office of Budget Responsibility had forecast.[15] The Bank of England reported that by the end of September the economy had already recovered nearly 90 per cent of its losses.[16]

Controlling its own currency and economy, the UK can borrow cheaply, increase the supply of money, and reduce taxes. In the short term this can sustain the economy and consumption, even during lockdown and its aftermath, and provide for investment too. The sums involved seem frightening and beyond normal comprehension, but they are far from unprecedented. At the end of the Napoleonic Wars in 1815, the national debt was 250 per cent of gross national income, and after the First World War over 300 per cent.[17] The COVID crisis is bringing the national debt up to around 100 per cent of GDP, but over a third of this is held by the Bank of England and involves no interest payments. Conventionally, such debts are managed by a mixture of economic growth, austerity, default or inflation – preferably by the first of these, which requires prosperity-creating policies of education, training and investment over the next generation. Paradoxically, the main danger would be a panicky attempt to reduce the deficit by austerity – too hastily cutting expenditure or raising taxes. For a sovereign country following sensible policies, much of this necessary debt never has to be repaid and is, therefore, not a burden on the future.

With COVID and culture wars dominating the headlines, Brexit had seemingly been relegated to a pre-pandemic age. But negotiations between the UK and the EU on their future relationship were continuing. Britain's chief official negotiator was for the first time a genuine Brexiteer, David Frost, who spoke of 'the reappearance on the political scene not just of national feeling but also of the wish for national decision-making and the revival of the nation state' not only in Britain but across Europe: 'the EU must, if it is to achieve what it wants in the world, find a way of relating to its neighbours as friends and genuinely sovereign equals.'[18] It was not clear that the EU wanted such a relationship. It was now visibly alarmed that the UK might gain trading advantages once outside the EU, and demanded 'a level playing field' – not just the normal safeguards against unfair trade contained in all free trade agreements and in WTO rules, but rather that Britain would follow EU regulations both present and future, as interpreted by the European Court. The EU also demanded a continuation of the Common Fisheries Policy. This was from a Brexiteer point of view an absurdity, and the government said so.

Over the period from 2016 to 2020, the EU line had shifted, indeed reversed. At first, it had insisted that the UK as a 'third country' would be refused a special relationship ('cherry picking') and would be left 'very lonely on the edge of the Atlantic'.[19] But when the Johnson government said that third-country status was just what it wanted, the EU insisted that the UK must accept a special relationship, because of its 'economic interconnectedness and geographical proximity'.[20]

Frost, in a polite but forthright letter of 19 May, retorted that this 'is not an argument that can hope to be accepted in the 21st century'. Like a nineteenth-century imperial power, the EU was claiming a sphere of influence over the UK. Fishing rights, although in economic terms relatively minor, crystallized this difference of view: the UK considered that by leaving the EU it automatically regained sovereign rights over its coastal waters; but Brussels seemed to regard the UK as claiming something that belonged to the EU. It began to look as if the 'transition period' for negotiation might end without agreement in December 2020, after which the EU and the UK would conduct their commercial relations under basic World Trade Organization rules. How much on both sides was bluff? The British government seemed now resolved to say no if necessary, and had prepared to trade on WTO terms, with a few ad hoc arrangements in addition. The EU seemed equally determined: in Michel Barnier's inimitable Eurospeak, '*C'est naturellement un no-go*.'[21] The Irish border continued to raise difficulties, and unless a free trade agreement with the EU was signed, the UK was obliged under the Withdrawal Agreement to create something like an economic frontier between Northern Ireland and Great Britain. The British government promised to waive customs declarations or checks on goods going from Northern Ireland to Great Britain, and in the other direction HM Revenue and Customs itself was instructed to facilitate the formalities free of charge. But the legal problem remained.

From May 2020 onwards there was a tangible revival of Remainer activity in Britain, which gathered momentum during the autumn. Media articles appeared urging an extension to the 'transition period' during which Britain was half in and half out of the EU. Barnier accused the UK of backsliding from promises he said it had made in the now famous Political Declaration, and suggested extending the transition period by 'one or two years'. This was turned down by the British government, and the deadline for requesting an extension to the transition period passed on 30 June, almost unnoticed. A different tactic appeared. Familiar alarms about 'chlorinated chicken' and hormones in beef were revived to raise obstacles to trade agreements, especially with the United States. Putting off Britain's final departure, keeping its financial contributions going as long as possible (including possible contributions to a COVID bailout), doing everything to prevent it from competing effectively with the EU, impeding its trade with other countries, and keeping the notoriously pugnacious French and Spanish farmers and fishermen happy were all eminently desirable objects for Brussels. The mystery is why anybody in the UK should want to go along with them. The explanation is a wish to string the process out, to block trade agreements with other countries (talks were underway with Japan, the USA, Australia, New Zealand, Switzerland and Canada), and so keep Britain dependent on the EU in the hope that we might one day drift back. Given the crisis facing the EU, which even the keenest Rejoiners must have been dimly aware of, these activities were, to put it mildly, disingenuous.

From September to November, negotiations with the EU reached a rather frenetic climax. This was partly the expected pattern as successive deadlines for agreement (announced by both sides) approached. The temperature was further raised by the introduction on 9 September of an Internal Market Bill. This broadly embodied intentions announced in January 2019 by Theresa May to protect internal UK trade between Northern Ireland and Great Britain in case of failure to conclude a free trade agreement with the EU. But now controversy was sparked when the Northern Ireland secretary read a prepared statement in the Commons saying that the Bill would 'break international law in a very specific and limited way' by overriding (or interpreting) the terms of the Northern Ireland Protocol. Outrage, real or feigned, was expressed by EU politicians – who peremptorily summoned Johnson to withdraw the Bill – and by many British Remainers, who, as ever, sided with the EU. Brexiteer lawyers argued that the Bill was in fact justifiable under international law, both because the Protocol was contradictory and because the EU was not negotiating in good faith. So why was the government saying the opposite? What was '*le jeu obscure de la perfide Albion*', as one French newspaper put it?[22] Many theories emerged: ministerial stupidity; civil service duplicity; tough tactics with Brussels; forestalling accusations that the House had been misled; perhaps even provoking the EU into breaking off negotiations so that the whole unsatisfactory Withdrawal Agreement could be dumped by a formal procedure of 'denunciation'. Despite its professed indignation, the EU continued to negotiate: the stakes for its exporters were too high, and the advantages the Withdrawal Agreement gave it not to be risked lightly. These included an obligation on the UK to accept the jurisdiction of the European Court for four years, as well as other 'enforcement' procedures favouring the EU.

By the end of October, the negotiations at times appeared on the point of breakdown, and then suddenly seemed to regain impetus – the usual choreography of EU politics. There were three outstanding issues. Fishing rights were emotive but technical, depending on quotas and future negotiations, and hence open to compromise. Rules on state aid to industry in principle were negotiable; but that really depended on the extent to which the EU wanted to assert control over future British economic policy on the grounds that Britain was uniquely integrated with Europe, and that it feared the creation of what it called 'Singapore on Thames'. This was also the case with the so-called 'level playing field': Barnier said he wanted to prevent the UK from becoming a 'manufacturing hub' on the EU's doorstep.[23] Agreements over fair trading practices are contained in all trade agreements and in WTO rules, but the EU demanded much wider powers to judge and retaliate against anything it considered unfair, and to change the rules as it saw fit, without conceding reciprocal rights to the UK. France seemed to be taking the hardest line, despite its relatively weak position. Other member states with much to lose seemed to favour compromise. Which side was really making concessions was opaque even to seeming insiders, given the theatrical nature of the negotiations. The election of the anti-Brexit and ostensibly pro-Irish Joe Biden to the American presidency in early November added another element of uncertainty. So did the sudden removal on the 13th of Dominic Cummings from his position as the Prime Minister's chief advisor. Then on the 16th the EU began its own crisis, when Poland and Hungary vetoed the budget, including the 'historic' COVID rescue package, only three days before a meeting of the European Council said to be making a final decision on a deal with Britain. But the 19th passed with nothing being decided or even discussed. An EU negotiator developed COVID, a pretext for further postponement. Neither side, it seemed, wished to give ground or to take responsibility for breaking off the talks. Whether or not there was to be a last-minute agreement on trade before the end of the year, the tug of war threatened to continue.

How the Eurozone faces up to the economic and financial aftermath of COVID will be a subject of international concern for years. Even if it avoids disaster, much of it faces economic stagnation for the foreseeable future. Political tensions seem inevitable. If there is a serious financial crisis in 2021, no part of the world will completely escape the effects, and certainly not our islands. The pandemic might in theory have galvanized the EU into improvising a workable confederation based on a suddenly realized European solidarity. This would have begun by raising an adequate fund to sustain damaged economies which, not being in control of their currencies, are dependent on joint action. Instead, it exposed the national, cultural and economic tensions behind the gold-spangled banner.

In Britain, too, the combination of Brexit, COVID, international instability and domestic discontent constituted a formidable short- and long-term challenge to the Johnson government. The mediocre response to the COVID crisis re-emphasized the need for a shake-up: arguably, the whole system of government had been sluggish, displaying the disadvantages of centralization without the advantages.[24] Yet opportunities as well as risks arose both from Brexit and from the COVID crisis – new supply chains, new trading patterns, new international partners, new methods of working, even new industries. Government needed to further these, as much as cushioning the pre-Brexit and pre-COVID economy. The first steps have been to announce a large programme of public spending on hospitals, schools, houses, and other infrastructure. 'Schools and hospitals' are always vote-winners. More difficult is improving what goes on inside them. House-building helped us out of the 1930s slump, but it does not help to balance our enormous external trade deficit.

Domestically, the problems were not new, but the economic damage of the COVID crisis made social and regional 'levelling up' both more urgent and more difficult. Coastal districts and some Northern and Midland towns had still not found satisfactory replacements for their old industries. With an end to free movement from Europe, and the adoption (if carried out effectively) of a controlled immigration system, labour becomes less plentiful and less cheap. There will at last be a strong incentive for governments and businesses to invest seriously in education and training, and to bring about a regional 'levelling up' that will not merely be a political sop but an economic necessity. The weakness of vocational training in the UK has long been recognized and lamented, but now it is in everyone's interest to remedy it. There were some hopeful signs: following the Augar Review of further education in May 2019,[25] the government announced in September 2020 increased and more flexible financial support for adult education and training. It will also become advantageous to invest in improving productivity – for some years a British problem. Employees should become a valuable resource to be cherished, not a disposable commodity.

The COVID crisis has altered, possibly for good, everyday working practices. Suddenly, old technologies (and egregiously the HS2 railway project, Keynesianism at its crudest) seem absurd when new communication technologies abolish distance. To what extent new patterns of working will become permanent, whether they will disperse activity and wealth away from London, and whether they will increase or lessen productivity is unclear. In any case, the economic and financial devastation suffered makes it urgent for the UK to be as efficient, integrated and resilient as possible. Instead of the old leviathans of heavy industry, the most dynamic and forward-looking parts of the economy are often small companies engaged in services, the 'digital economy', specialized manufacturing and high-quality agriculture. Consequently, the government's main tasks are to provide cultural capital, infrastructure, fiscal encouragement, a realistic energy policy, favourable political conditions and global trading relationships. In September 2020, the post-Brexit City of London was judged to be catching up with New York as the world's main financial centre; no EU city was in the top ten.[26]

Leaving the EU requires strategic choices that the UK would have had to face in one way or another sooner or later. The hope that the EU could provide a counterweight to the superpowers and a bulwark against global dangers was always part of the European dream, but it was never wanted or believed in by most people in the UK. The EU has no significant military or diplomatic power because only a tiny minority of its peoples see this as a priority and its member states have few shared aims. Its elaborate foreign policy apparatus is 'a substitute for real action'.[27] French ambitions for a European army have so far materialized as 95 Estonians, 60 Czechs and 2 Danes assisting its 5,000 troops in Africa.[28] Equally patent is the EU's inaction over tensions in the eastern Mediterranean involving Greece, France, Italy and Turkey – in theory, a candidate for membership.[29] It is still NATO, not the EU, that guarantees European peace. As a senior American diplomat had predicted more than a decade ago:

the European Union is likely in coming years to be a theoretically powerful but crisis-prone second-rate power caught in an unending geopolitical tug-of-war between other poles in the international system . . . [It] is likely to resemble not 19th-century Britain or Germany, but their palsied polyglot neighbor, the Austro-Hungarian Empire.[30]

Will post-Brexit Britain prioritize the security of Eastern Europe, the Mediterranean, Asia or Africa? The forthcoming Strategic Defence and Security Review will be a crucial indication. Important decisions have already been made, notably to combine the Foreign and Commonwealth Office and the Department for International Development to enable a more ambitious national strategy, rather than aiming merely to be a good member of the club. The disinterestedness of Britain's previous development policy had been admired by other countries, but they had not been tempted to emulate it. A new approach will require a change of attitude and perhaps of personnel. In October 2020, the House of Commons Foreign Affairs Select Committee reported that Britain's foreign policy was lacking in clarity, confidence, strategic vision and presence on the world stage, and its diplomacy was risk-averse.[31] The appointment of David Frost as National Security Adviser from August 2020 signalled a new direction.

The existence of an economically powerful and externally assertive China, a politically confused and divided USA, an impotent and inward-looking EU, a reckless and disruptive Russia (never as strong or as weak as it seems, as Churchill noted), and the challenge of dealing rationally with climate change and its multiple consequences – all create a newly uncertain world. A fundamental duty of the government is to ensure that Brexit is not a further element of global vulnerability, as some in Russia and China apparently hope, but that Britain plays a more effective role in strengthening the security of the democratic world. A greedy and inattentive West has facilitated the growth of Chinese power. Despite its being a cruel, unscrupulous and ambitious dictatorship, too many governments and institutions turned a blind eye, tempted by naïve hopes of economic partnership. The Chinese state was able to establish influential positions within European countries and their institutions. These include the UK,[32] which has allowed penetration by a potentially hostile state to a degree unparalleled since Charles II accepted money and mistresses from Louis XIV. This reality is dawning on the public and politicians.

As if to underline the point, China's rulers went on an alarming rampage during the summer of 2020. The nature and degree of its responsibility for the COVID pandemic aroused suspicion, but, when Australia proposed an international investigation, China applied economic sanctions. In Hong Kong, using the crisis as camouflage, Beijing began its final suppression of liberty, a contemptuous abrogation of the Hong Kong Basic Law and a blatant challenge to post-Brexit Britain. It was met by courageous demonstrations in Hong Kong and protests by the United States, Britain, Australia and New Zealand – though significantly not by the EU. The United Kingdom, with other Commonwealth countries, promised to facilitate the entry of Overseas UK passport holders from the former colony, which again provoked Chinese anger – one petty act of revenge seems to have been China's pressure on Barbados to renounce the Queen as Head of State. In June

Australia experienced cyberattacks that clearly originated in China. On the Ladakh frontier, twenty unarmed Indian soldiers were ambushed and murdered by Chinese troops. Tensions were raised with Japan and other maritime neighbours over territorial waters. The habitual threats were made to Taiwan. Then in quick succession in July and August, the Chinese government concluded long-term oil and gas contracts with Iran (for $400 billion – effectively a monopsony for twenty-five years), Saudi Arabia (it is said in exchange for nuclear technologies that the USA would not provide), and Abu Dhabi, securing long-term supplies at bargain prices at the expense of Europe and Japan. Significantly, these militantly Islamic countries are unmoved by China's totalitarian treatment of its Muslim Uighur population. Moreover, this pre-emption of vast oil supplies, combined with massive use of coal for electricity generation, suggests how far Beijing's vaunted backing of Green technology is a weapon against a gullible West.

Where will the post-Brexit UK stand in this shifting world order? For the time being, circumstances are aligning it with its Anglophone allies of the 'Five Eyes' intelligence network. Use of the Chinese corporation Huawei's 5G communications equipment, previously agreed by the May government with the encouragement of highly placed establishment figures in Chinese employ, became a test. Following Australia and the United States, and in turn followed by France, Johnson resolved to ignore threats from Beijing and exclude Huawei from future communications systems. Britain has, furthermore, proposed forming a 'D10 group' of democracies to develop secure communications technology, including the large European countries, the USA, Canada, Japan,

Australia, India and South Korea, which has been described as 'a golden opportunity for London to put some meat on the bones on the still unproven "Global Britain" concept'.[33]

Though the UK has troops in Estonia to deter Russian adventures, and a few in Mali to help the French, a more striking development has been to raise its profile 'East of Suez'. In 2019 it stationed a frigate and several mine countermeasures warships at its naval base in Bahrain. It is likely to send the new aircraft carrier *Queen Elizabeth* for her first deployment in 2021 to the Far East, possibly for joint manoeuvres with the USA, Australia and Japan. These countries have already been contesting Beijing's claims to control the South China Sea by exercising legal rights of passage, and the Royal Navy may again participate, as it did in 2018. Will this be paralleled by economic links through the Trans-Pacific Partnership, which the United States might also join? All this will certainly further anger the Chinese, and it places British policy in a different sphere from that of the EU.

But, for the moment, the needs are closer to home: controlling COVID, reviving the economy, agreeing a sensible relationship with the EU, pursuing new trade links (that with Japan is the first, signed on 23 October), adopting an acceptable immigration system, and soothing our domestic squabbles. Nearly all historians agree that one should 'never prophesy, especially about the future'. Bold predictions usually turn out wrong, or mistimed, or self-evident. But in the final section of this book, which is not only a history, I shall attempt a few.

Conclusion: 'Not in Our Stars'

'Europe as we had imagined it is finished. The Europe we wanted we shall never see.'
François Hollande, president of the French Republic,
after the Brexit referendum, 2016[1]

'I don't think the EU is capable of doing anything to us other than harm. I opposed Brexit but I have now reached the conclusion that the British did the right thing, even if they did it for the wrong reason.'
Yanis Varoufakis, former Greek
finance minister, March 2020[2]

The Brexit years felt historic to those living through them, and so they were. But will they be more than a footnote in history? Many seemingly momentous events fade from memory. The long struggle over free trade, which remade our politics in the 1840s and again in the 1900s, is now a subject for specialists. How many people brood over the disastrous decline in the 1920s of the Liberal Party, which had dominated Victorian England? Does the failure of the League of Nations in the 1930s keep anyone awake at night? Perhaps in a few years the new generation will wonder why people got so worked up about Brexit. Let us hope so: it is violence and disaster that long remain in the collective memory, and Brexit has brought no violence and there is no sign of disaster.

How might Brexit be remembered in Britain, as far as it is

remembered at all? At least as an alteration in economic and political direction after nearly fifty years of hesitant commitment to European integration. At best, as the beginning of an effort to improve social cohesion, to shake up a tired system of government, and to reset an exhausted national strategy. At worst, as the acceleration of a long decline into relative poverty, global marginalization, and social and political disintegration. This third possibility is the standard Remainer scenario, which some cling to with fierce passion. Which of these turns out to be true depends partly on the state of a suddenly unstable world, but, above all, on our collective decisions: 'The fault, dear Brutus, is not in our stars, but in ourselves.'

Though it sparked a 'culture war', Brexit was essentially political. Most Leave voters of all classes were determined to have a government that would pay attention to them. Though often dismissed as populism, having governments that pay attention is the aim and constant effort of democracy. Not all Leavers want the same things, but they do want that, as traditional Labour voters showed in December 2019 by backing a Conservative government. Many people across Europe also want more political control. Yanis Varoufakis, long a prominent advocate of a democratized EU, now thinks that we did the right thing, if for the wrong reason. Those of us who supported Leave thought it was for the right reason: to reassert democracy in the only form in which it flourishes or has ever flourished – within a nation state. Many who voted Remain accept this view.

Brexit put strains on the political system itself. For a time there was a danger to a fundamental principle: that a legal vote is respected. The principle was vindicated, though fairly narrowly. The problem arose from an influential section of the elite seemingly being loyal to an outside institution (not the first time this has happened, but certainly the first time on such a scale for centuries). This may now decline. But mistrust and anger have accumulated about the legitimacy of the House of Lords and the Supreme Court, about the composition and representativeness of the political class as a whole, about the trustworthiness of the Electoral Commission, and about the impartiality of the BBC. It may be that this crisis has reshaped politics for the long term. One plausible future would see a hegemonic one-nation Conservative Party appealing to national identity and espousing more interventionist economics; an opposition composed of a Labour and/or Lib Dem Party based in a few cities and university towns and able to win up to about 170 seats;[3] plus a constellation of smaller parties, including nationalist and Green.

There was a paradox in Britain's relationship with the EU. We were not full members of all its institutions (crucially the single currency) and, as Remainers often argued, we were less affected by its failures. But because we were not full members, we were able to leave, unlike countries that were seriously damaged by membership but felt they had no choice but to remain. Why then, asked Remainers, go to the trouble of leaving? One reason is that the EU itself was changing, trying to move towards the greater centralization that supporters believed essential to its survival. This made Britain's semi-detached position less tenable, while only a tiny minority of its citizens wanted 'more Europe'.

Remainers often asked too what Leavers would do with the 'control' they had taken back. The full answer is that Brexit 'requires the construction of a completely new national economic and political settlement – one that will be thrashed out between the social classes, the leading sectors of the economy, and the nations and regions of the United Kingdom.'[4] That thrashing out is what democracy is for. The COVID crisis made it all the more urgent, as the old aims of unlimited globalization and/or European integration were both dissolving. John Gray argues that 'the era of peak globalisation is over . . . A more fragmented world is coming into being that in some ways may be more resilient.'[5] Britain must decide its response in a way it could not previously do.

The legal, political and economic arguments for leaving or remaining were obscured by the 'culture war', in which feelings of identity (at least for the most committed minorities on each side) came into play. Time will tell how wide the division really was, and to what extent it has been resolved by Brexit and a realignment of politics. Unless the EU experiences a miraculous transfiguration, a campaign to Rejoin cannot convince more than a minority of Ideological and Professional Remainers. If the UK continues to diversify trade and trading agreements outside the EU, rejoining would be an irrational act of self-harm. In the long run, it seems unlikely that most people will regard the turmoil of 2016–19 as something to be prolonged or revisited. The Leave–Remain division will therefore wane. Yet the emotions arising from identity politics will be with us for some time, perhaps in different forms.

The Union will certainly be contested, and vehemently so. The 2016 vote dramatized existing differences. Nationalists hope Brexit will push these to breaking point, leading to independence for Scotland and reunification for Ireland. But in practical terms, Brexit, unless it proves a disaster, makes Scottish independence dauntingly unfeasible and Irish unity unattractive. Scotland's fiscal deficit (sustained by the UK as a whole) is around £4,000 per household, and due to the COVID crisis may triple next year.[6] The financial burdens imposed by the EU on Ireland in 2009 and now again in 2020 should be a warning to Europhile nationalists: Ireland has ended up well ahead of Germany as the second largest per capita contributor to EU budgets. In the foreseeable future, most people in these islands will probably continue to accept the Union as the only plausible system. But will it be loved? There will remain a nagging discontent among nationalists, and a potentially dangerous feeling in England that it is hard done by – 'Who in England really cares about the union with Scotland?'[7] The present system of devolution of power within the UK does not at the moment seem stable and equitable. Advocates of constitutional reform have not yet achieved political prominence, but they may in due course emerge. In the longer term, Brexit should not be a threat to the Union. On the contrary, the more its opportunities are taken, the more the Union is strengthened and made attractive.

How might Brexit be remembered elsewhere? It has been mostly reported on the Continent and in Ireland in hostile, even apocalyptic, terms. That Britain has not yet collapsed economically and politically is a cause of perplexity, even disappointment. How Europeans feel about us has been affected. A poll in August 2020 asking people whether they would favour giving help to a country in crisis found the British willing to help every EU country (though even more willing to help Anglophone countries); but most EU countries would not be willing to help Britain.[8]

Brexit is a major blow to the European project, economically, politically, strategically and psychologically – something about which many people in Europe and beyond still seem in denial. Yet Brexit has at the same time been a warning of the domestic and international tensions that leaving the EU involves, and this has sharply increased acceptance of membership among its citizens. Brexit could spur a smaller EU, freed of its most sceptical member, towards greater centralization – the Macron vision of a 'sovereign Europe'.[9] Or Brexit could be the tolling bell, the first popular rejection that could not be reversed or ignored. In either case, it makes the fissures in the EU more visible. 'More Europe' will increase political and economic stresses. Talking about 'sovereignty', as Macron and others now do, raises a potentially dangerous issue: will the peoples of Europe acquiesce in an undisguised loss of national and democratic sovereignty? The assumption that they will do so indefinitely because they have no choice is a fragile basis for a great political enterprise, flying in the face of Europe's history and its vaunted values.

Should we, as a nation, be ashamed of disrupting the 'Europe' we insistently clamoured to join sixty years ago and have done our best to shape – some would say, to spoil? I don't think we have been 'perfidious Albion': not this time anyway. We tried to dissuade the EU from rushing into the single currency, its most disastrous adventure. We tried to moderate its dangerously undemocratic centralizing ambitions. We backed its rather ineffective diplomatic efforts while trying at the same time to hold NATO together. We spent a vast amount of money on helping to defend it, largely unacknowledged. We obeyed its flood of regulations rather more quickly than most other member states. We paid up year after year, relatively uncomplainingly, to subsidize our neighbours. The glad confident morning of European

integration had passed well before 2016: Brexit was a consequence, not a cause.

The idea of a united Europe as the embodiment and
defender of a certain humane civilization, even as an 'empire',
has attracted people for over 150 years – 'not so much a place
as an idea'.[10] The 'founding fathers' are seen by some as having
engaged in 'a heroic endeavour',[11] with its prime justification
the renunciation of chauvinism and war in favour of harmony,
friendship and the defence of European exceptionalism. Beet-
hoven's 'Ode to Joy' is an inspiring prophecy: 'All men will
be brothers . . .' The beguiling vision remains eternally just
over the horizon. Brexit was felt by many in Europe and Britain to be a philistine act of destruction, like smashing a Greek
statue or throwing acid over a Renaissance painting. But this
Europe, as Tony Judt pointed out, was 'a Europe of the mind'.[12]
As such, it enthused many intellectuals. But, despite huge and
continuing efforts, it has not managed to become equally
attractive as a Europe of realities, able to inspire the instinct-
ive shared identity that any democratic system – or even an
empire – requires to be successful. The only justification for
being willing to sacrifice our own democratic independence
and material interests to this faltering utopia would be if it did
indeed have some overriding political and moral purpose as
'a Europe of citizens, peoples, democracy and destiny'.[13] To
be frank, this is what Milan Kundera called political kitsch,
something the EU has been brilliant at creating. The reality is a rather cynical system in which some social groups,
some interests and some countries gain hugely, and others lose
hugely. If the EU one day succeeds in surmounting its formidable economic and political divisions, then it might seem in
retrospect that the British people should have been willing to

sacrifice their democratic sovereignty and economic security to be part of it. But I doubt it.

The worm in the bud has been perennial mistrust of democracy – a tragic irony given that universal democracy is the pinnacle (only just completed) of Europe's long political saga. The two world wars, in reality caused by authoritarian regimes, were wrongly blamed on the peoples of Europe. Their choices were therefore to be directed and their national identity neutered, despite this having been the strongest defence against the universalist totalitarianism of Nazism and communism. The enlightened elite – from Monnet and Schuman, via Delors, Mitterrand and Kohl to Juncker and Macron – circumvented what they saw as unenlightened democracy and hustled the peoples towards their destiny as good Europeans, just as Bavarians and Saxons had been made into Germans, and Tuscans and Sicilians into Italians. I have always been suspicious of the d'Azeglio formula (see above, p. 70), which copies nineteenth-century nationalism on a larger scale. It was dangerous in the 1850s. It is dangerous now. Dangerous for global economic stability.[14] Dangerous in undermining democratic governments. The adoption of the single currency, decided in the 1980s, was the point of no return: intended to pave the way for federation, it created deep and, so far, unbridgeable divisions. It was mainly a French initiative with the very traditional aim of controlling Germany: possibly the last time that France will direct Europe – a remarkable diplomatic and political achievement, but in the end a pyrrhic victory.

Even if it worked, would the effort to 'make Europeans' prove beneficial? The protection offered by national communities is precious, especially for the less privileged. As the economist Paul Collier explains:

the potential for European identity to *substitute* for national identity has profound consequences for the poorer citizens of Europe's nations. For them, the post-war sense of shared national identity had become a hugely valuable asset. Post-1980, just as the new economic forces of social divergence were necessitating national solidarity, this sense of shared identity was being unwound. The most successful citizens, namely the well-educated metropolitans who have enjoyed rising relative incomes, have gradually peeled off from shared national identity. The option of being 'European' has perhaps been a convenient justification for them to withdraw from obligations to their provincial fellow citizens.[15]

This secessionism of the wealthy can be seen clearly in Catalonia, Flanders, northern Italy and London.

Had the EU been economically successful, its peoples might perhaps have reconciled themselves to becoming denationalized Europeans under a technocracy with a systemic democratic deficit. After all, democracy is new and fragile in much of Europe, and is often tainted with failure and corruption. But the EU has not been successful, and it is now similarly tainted. Its defenders would perhaps argue that, without the EU, things would be worse – that we are 'better together'. Indeed, EU membership once buttressed democracy and the rule of law, as in Spain, Portugal and Greece, and in newly independent Eastern Europe. But now the biggest problems stem from the EU itself. It has created a political void between citizens and those who govern them: powers of decision have been removed from open electoral politics and placed in the shadowy realm of secret diplomacy.[16] The EU has become a political black hole, sucking authority away from elected governments but being unable to wield that authority effectively. It faces a series of problems it cannot solve: migration, unemployment, and the growing inequalities and dangers of the Eurozone system. Its ambition to play a superpower role falls embarrassingly short. Its response to the COVID pandemic, which seems to many a make-or-break challenge, has again underlined its divisions and limitations.

Even people who accept many of these criticisms fall back on an ultimate argument of political gigantism: the EU is very big; and post-Brexit Britain is small. Versions of this argument are more than a century old. Its core assumption was first put forward by Joseph Chamberlain before the First World War: 'The days are for great empires, not for little states.' He was bizarrely echoed by the European Parliament's Brexit co-ordinator Guy Verhofstadt: 'The world order of tomorrow is not . . . based on nation states or countries. It is a world order that is based on empires.'[17] Whether this is truer now than it was in 1903 is questionable: the empires of Chamberlain's day have all gone, and the nations remain. Do Verhofstadt's empires look a better bet today? Where would you choose to face a pandemic: Singapore or China? Where would you put your life savings: Switzerland or the Eurozone? Brexit is undoubtedly a gamble on the democratic nation state, its viability and its future, but one informed by British and European history and culture. The EU is a greater gamble, for it defies both history and culture, and its size may be its downfall. John Gray comments that 'the progressive mind detests national identity with passionate intensity . . . But the nation state is increasingly the most powerful force driving large-scale action.'[18]

The EU's less-than-stable political and economic system raises new problems for the UK. But it also alleviates one very old problem: how to manage relations with the Continent. A central tenet of British foreign policy over the last 500 years has been to prevent a potential enemy from dominating Europe. This was one of the reasons for applying to join the Common Market in the 1960s: fear that a United States of Europe without Britain might be a threat. The reality today is very different: a European Union that is weak and divided, but which restrains its member states from dangerous actions. So the UK can safely withdraw – at least for now. It could retire into relative isolation and political quietism, as William Waldegrave has suggested, giving up its UN Security Council seat, its nuclear submarines and its aircraft carriers: 'Get real! Be a medium-sized, wealthy, well-run modern nation.'[19] But if it does not do this – and its long-held position as one of the world's half-dozen or so most powerful states makes it unlikely – then it must look for an alternative strategy to that of European integration. Of course, Britain will continue to co-operate with European states when necessary, particularly France, the only one of them with the means and will to act beyond its borders. In particular, Britain has an interest in resisting the growing influence Russia exercises in Europe both by intimidation and by control of energy supplies. We would certainly be ready, if the need arose, to help build a post-federalist Europe of co-operating nations. Meanwhile, there is, of course, a very obvious alternative: the so-called 'Anglosphere'.[20]

This has been venomously attacked as neo-imperialist nostalgia. But nostalgia is a longing for something that no longer exists, and it applies at least as aptly to the faded dream of a

United States of Europe. Let us consider twenty-first-century realities. Germany has just set out a future Indo-Pacific policy. President Macron, champion of the EU though he is, recently declared that 'The 20th century was continental . . . The 21st century will be oceanic. That is where the power and geopolitics of tomorrow are being played out.' It would be a strange irony if Britain allowed itself to remain tied to a declining Continent while France embraced a global future as what Macron calls 'Europe's leading maritime power . . . in global partnership . . . with our friends Australia, Japan and India'.[21]

There are among English-speaking countries important shared memories, including memories that divide as well as some that unite. Sentiment aside, language, similarity of legal systems and robust attachment to democracy create strong connections. Despite America's present turmoil, it will remain the core of both Atlantic and Pacific security systems and the hub of the world economy. In the view of one Hungarian scholar (unlikely to be nostalgic for the pomp of the Raj), Brexit will probably tighten existing trade, cultural and security links that 'upgrade the status of the Anglosphere'. This would

> combine the strength of British and US navies and nuclear arsenals, food security granted by combined capacity of the Australian, Canadian and US agricultures, energy security granted by combined oil and natural gas reserves of Canada and the US as well as by combined uranium reserves of Australia, Canada and the US, military presence not only in Europe, North America and Australasia, but also through the network of US and UK military bases all over the world.[22]

Within such a system, the Commonwealth – which a relatively small number of people, notably the Queen, have kept alive – provides 'soft power' based on the affection in which it is manifestly held by so many of its citizens. It can help support and attract fragile but important countries now threatened by predatory forces, especially if British foreign aid is in future used purposefully. Relations with India will also be significant. Perhaps all of this will never happen, or not in this form. But some of it certainly will, and the sudden spectre of Chinese expansionism may give it impetus.

Geography comes before history. But for centuries we have been loosening the bonds of time and distance. Place has become less important. Language and culture, shaped by history, have become more so. Far from being a step into the past, leaving the EU demands fresh engagement with the twenty-first century, offering both dangers and opportunities. How Britain responds, and how well it succeeds, will make it an example for others to follow, or for others to avoid.

Acknowledgements

I would like to give my sincere thanks to those of diverse political views who were kind enough to respond to requests for information or to make other suggestions, and in some cases even to read and comment on sections of the text: Anna Bailey, Neema Begum, David Blake, Sir John Curtice, Robin Dunbar, Richard Ekins, Matthew Elliott, Leigh Evans, Evelyn Farr, Matthew Goodwin, Graham Gudgin, Rt Hon. David Jones MP, John Keiger, Ann Louise Kinmonth, John Longworth, Noel Malcolm, Charles Moore, Richard Nolan, Ian Park, Helen Parr, Gwythian Prins, John Ranelagh, Adam Slater, Nick Wood, and the little platoon of *Briefings for Brexit/Briefings for Britain*. My wife, Isabelle, one of *le dernier carré* of Remainers, showed admirable forbearance, and even kindly read (and criticized) Chapter 4. Thanks and apologies to anyone I may inadvertently have omitted. All opinions expressed are, of course, mine. Bill Hamilton, my agent, was unfailingly encouraging, and Stuart Proffitt edited the text with his habitual discernment and courtesy. I am pretty sure that neither of them agrees with me over Brexit, and so I am doubly grateful that neither has allowed this to ruffle our cordial professional and personal relations. I have long been in the debt of the whole team at Penguin, a model publisher. Finally, I would like warmly to thank academic colleagues, in my own college, St John's, and beyond, who have given encouragement, and people from Britain and abroad, nearly all previously unknown to me, who have written spontaneously at various times over the last four years to express support.

Notes

PREFACE

1. Charles de Gaulle, *Mémoires d'Espoir* (Paris, Plon, 1970), p. 203 (my translation).

I. SET IN A SILVER SEA

1. Jonathan Scott, *When the Waves Ruled Britannia* (Cambridge, Cambridge University Press, 2011), p. 139.
2. Jonathan Scott, *England's Troubles: Seventeenth-Century English Political Instability in European Context* (Cambridge, Cambridge University Press, 2000), p. 10.
3. The great work is N. A. M. Rodger's ongoing Naval History of Britain. On invasions, see vol. I, *The Safeguard of the Sea* (London, Penguin, 2004), p. 429.
4. Ibid., p. 427.
5. Robert Bartlett, *The Making of Europe: Conquest, Colonization and Cultural Change, 950–1350* (London, Penguin, 1994).
6. Tony Claydon, *Europe and the Making of England, 1660–1760* (Cambridge, Cambridge University Press, 2007).
7. Scott, *When the Waves Ruled Britannia*, p. 120.
8. Niall Ferguson, *The Cash Nexus: Money and Power in the Modern World 1700–2000* (London, Allen Lane, 2001), pp. 29–37, 426.
9. Scott, *England's Troubles*, p. 7.
10. N. A. M. Rodger, *The Command of the Ocean* (London, Penguin, 2006), p. lxv.

11. Boyd Hilton, *A Mad, Bad and Dangerous People? England 1783–1846* (Oxford, Clarendon Press, 2006), p. 557.

12. The judgement of a senior officer in 1899. G. R. Searle, *A New England? Peace and War, 1886–1918* (Oxford, Oxford University Press, 2004), p. 302.

13. John Bew, *Castlereagh: Enlightenment, War and Tyranny* (London, Quercus, 2011), p. 482.

14. Peter T. Marsh, *Bargaining on Europe: Britain and the First Common Market, 1860–1892* (London, Yale University Press, 1999).

15. Jürgen Osterhammel, *The Transformation of the World: A Global History of the Nineteenth Century* (Princeton, NJ, Princeton University Press, 2014), p. 460.

16. Christopher Clark, *The Sleepwalkers: How Europe Went to War in 1914* (London, Allen Lane, 2012), p. 493.

17. https://www.gov.uk/government/speeches/pm-speech-on-the-uks-strength-and-security-in-the-eu-9-may-2016.

18. The strongest argument is perhaps Niall Ferguson, *The Pity of War* (London, Penguin, 1999), pp. 168–73, 458–61.

19. John Charmley, *Chamberlain and the Lost Peace* (London, Hodder & Stoughton, 1989); Robert Crowcroft, *The End is Nigh: British Politics, Power and the Road to the Second World War* (Oxford, Oxford University Press, 2019).

20. Luisa Passerini, *Europe in Love, Love in Europe: Imagination and Politics between the Wars* (New York, State University of New York Press, 1999), p. 234 and *passim*; Andrea Bosco, *June 1940, Great Britain and the First Attempt to Build a European Union* (Newcastle upon Tyne, Cambridge Scholars Publishing, 2016).

21. Churchill in the House of Commons, 14 March 1933, quoted in David Cannadine and Ronald Quinault, eds., *Winston Church-*

ill in the Twenty-First Century (Cambridge, Cambridge University Press, 2004), p. 170.

22. Fundamental reinterpretations of the war are Phillips Payson O'Brien, *How the War was Won: Air–Sea Power and Allied Victory in World War II* (Cambridge, Cambridge University Press, 2015) and Evan Mawdsley, *The War for the Seas: A Maritime History of World War II* (New Haven and London, Yale University Press, 2019).

23. *The Times*, 12 Apr. 2018.

24. D. Sriskandarajah and C. Drew, 'Brits abroad: mapping the scale and nature of British emigration', Institute for Public Policy Research, 2006.

2. JOINING 'EUROPE'

1. 'Appel du 18 janvier', quoted in Tony Corn, *'Finis Austriae, Finis Europae?'* L'Europe post-Brexit et le syndrome austro-hongrois', Academia, 2020, p. 12 (my translation), https://www.academia.edu/42681691/Finis_Austriae_Finis_Europae_LEurope_post_Brexit_et_le_syndrome_austro_hongrois.

2. Sir Con O'Neill, *Britain's Entry into the European Community*, ed. D. Hannay (London, Frank Cass, 2000), p. xxii.

3. Alan Sharp and Glyn Stone, eds., *Anglo-French Relations in the Twentieth Century: Rivalry and Cooperation* (London, Routledge, 2000), p. 259.

4. Anthony Adamthwaite, *Britain, France and Europe, 1945–1975* (London, Bloomsbury, 2020).

5. Minute of meeting on 5 Jan. 1949, and memo of meeting on 23 Aug. 1950, quoted in Robert Tombs and Emile Chabal, eds., *Britain and France in Two World Wars: Truth, Myth and Memory* (London, Continuum, 2013), p. 206.

6. Alan S. Milward, *The UK and the European Community*, vol. I: *The Rise and Fall of a National Strategy, 1945–1963* (London, Frank Cass, 2002), p. 71.

7. Alan S. Milward, *The European Rescue of the Nation-State* (London, Routledge, 1992), p. 13.

8. Ibid., pp. 334–5.

9. Ibid., p. 17.

10. For details, see John Gillingham, *European Integration, 1950–2003: Superstate or New Market Economy?* (Cambridge, Cambridge University Press, 2003), pp. 22–33.

11. David Reynolds, *Island Stories: Britain and its History in the Age of Brexit* (London, William Collins, 2019), p. 109.

12. Milward, *The UK and the European Community*, vol. I, p. 3.

13. Ibid., pp. 317–18.

14. Jim Tomlinson, 'Thrice denied: "declinism" as a recurrent theme in British history in the long twentieth century', *Twentieth Century British History* 20 (2009), p. 235.

15. Milward, *The UK and the European Community*, vol. I, p. 251.

16. O'Neill, *Britain's Entry*, p. 355.

17. Sir Stephen Wall, *The Official History of Britain and the European Community*, vol. II: *From Rejection to Referendum, 1963–1975* (London, Routledge, 2013), p. 81, and see Helen Parr, *Britain's Policy towards the European Community: Harold Wilson and Britain's World Role, 1964–67* (London, Routledge, 2006).

18. Jim Tomlinson, 'Inventing "decline": the falling behind of the British economy in the postwar years', *Economic History Review* 49 (1996), p. 742.

19. *The Cambridge Economic History of Modern Britain*, ed. R. Floud and P. Johnson, vol. III (Cambridge, Cambridge University Press, 2004), p. 10.

20. Tomlinson, 'Thrice denied', p. 238.

21. The classic account for France is Jean Fourastié, *Les Trente Glorieuses, ou la révolution invisible de 1946 à 1975* (Paris, Fayard, 1979). For agricultural productivity, see p. 49.

22. A brilliant summary is Tomlinson, 'Thrice denied'.

23. Graham Gudgin and Ken Coutts, 'Did EU membership accelerate UK economic growth?' *Social Europe*, 29 September 2017, https://www.socialeurope.eu/eu-membership-accelerate-uk-economic-growth.

24. Gillingham, *European Integration*, p. 501.

25. O'Neill, *Britain's Entry*, p. 355.

26. Milward, *The UK and the European Community*, vol. I, pp. 317, 444.

27. A reasoned restatement is William Waldegrave, *Three Circles into One* (London, Mensch Publishing, 2019).

28. Avner Offer, 'Costs and benefits, prosperity and security, 1870–1914', in *The Oxford History of the British Empire*, vol. III: *The Nineteenth Century*, ed. A. Porter (London, Oxford University Press, 1999), p. 708.

29. Ronald Hyam, *Britain's Declining Empire* (Cambridge, Cambridge University Press, 2006), p. 74.

30. Alex May, ed., *Britain, the Commonwealth and Europe* (Houndmills, Palgrave, 2001), pp. 87–8.

31. Ashoka Mody, *EuroTragedy: A Drama in Nine Acts* (Oxford, Oxford University Press, 2018), p. 30.

32. Milward, *The UK and the European Community*, vol. I, p. 330.

33. May, ed., *Britain, the Commonwealth and Europe*, p. 103.

34. Ibid., p. 90.

35. Milward, *The UK and the European Community*, vol. I, p. 60.

36. De Gaulle jocularly denied using this phrase, but the political journalist Jean-Raymond Tournoux, who reported it, maintained that he had.

37. Parr, *Britain's Policy towards the European Community*, p. 103.

38. O'Neill, *Britain's Entry*, p. xiv.

39. For details, see Mody, *EuroTragedy*, pp. 36–42.

40. O'Neill, *Britain's Entry*, p. 40.

41. Sir Roy Denman, *Missed Chances: Britain and Europe in the Twentieth Century* (London, Indigo, 1997), p. 233.

42. Richard Weight, *Patriots: National Identity in Britain, 1940–2000* (London, Macmillan, 2002), pp. 477–82.

3. SECOND THOUGHTS

1. Ashoka Mody, *EuroTragedy: A Drama in Nine Acts* (Oxford, Oxford University Press, 2018), pp. 97–8.

2. Quoted in Charles Moore, *Margaret Thatcher: The Authorized Biography*, vol. III: *Herself Alone* (London, Allen Lane, 2019), p. 123.

3. Ed Jones, 'Commonwealth and EU growth', *World Economics Journal*, June 2018.

4. George L. Bernstein, *The Myth of Decline: The Rise of Britain since 1945* (London, Pimlico, 2004), p. 243.

5. Richard Vinen, *Thatcher's Britain: The Politics and Social Upheaval of the 1980s* (London, Simon & Schuster, 2009), p. 36; Peter Clarke, *Hope and Glory: Britain 1900–1990* (London, Allen Lane, 1996), p. 402.

6. Jim Tomlinson, 'Thrice denied: "declinism" as a recurrent theme in British history in the long twentieth century', *Twentieth Century British History* 20 (2009), p. 238.

7. Helen Parr, *Britain's Policy towards the European Community: Harold Wilson and Britain's World Role, 1964–67* (London, Routledge, 2006), p. 30.

8. Jean Rey, quoted in Roger Eatwell and Matthew Goodwin, *National Populism: The Revolt against Liberal Democracy* (London, Penguin, 2018), p. 99.

9. Hugo Young, *This Blessed Plot: Britain and Europe from Churchill to Blair* (London, Macmillan, 1998), pp. 290–91.

10. Sir Stephen Wall, *The Official History of Britain and the European Community*, vol. II: *From Rejection to Referendum, 1963–1975* (London, Routledge, 2013), pp. 585–90. See also Young, *Blessed Plot*, pp. 290–94.

11. Young, *Blessed Plot*, p. 290.

12. John Gillingham, *European Integration, 1950–2003: Superstate or New Market Economy?* (Cambridge, Cambridge University Press, 2003), pp. 136, 146.

13. Speech at The Hague, 1992. Margaret Thatcher Foundation, https://www.margaretthatcher.org/document/108296

14. Margaret Thatcher, *The Downing Street Years* (London, HarperCollins, 1993), p. 726.

15. Ibid., p. 727.

16. Dominique Strauss-Kahn, 'Building a political Europe: 50 proposals for tomorrow's Europe', April 2004, p. 105.

17. Philip Cunliffe, *The New Twenty Years' Crisis: A Critique of International Relations, 1999–2019* (London, McGill-Queen's University Press, 2020), pp. 108–9; Richard Tuck, *The Left Case for Brexit* (Cambridge, Polity Press, 2020), p. 113.

18. Larry Siedentop, *Democracy in Europe* (London, Allen Lane, 2000), p. 119.

19. George Ross, *Jacques Delors and European Integration* (Cambridge, Polity Press, 1995), p. 233.

20. Cris Shore, *Building Europe: The Cultural Politics of European Integration* (London, Routledge, 2000), p. 18.

21. 'The Bruges speech, 20 September 1988', Margaret Thatcher Foundation.

22. See notes on 'The Bruges speech, 20 September 1988', Margaret Thatcher Foundation.

23. Moore, *Margaret Thatcher*, vol. III, p. 507.

24. Mody, *EuroTragedy*, pp. 72–9.

25. Tony Judt, *A Grand Illusion? An Essay on Europe* (London, Penguin, 1997), p. 87.

26. Siedentop, *Democracy in Europe*, p. 134.

27. Joseph E. Stiglitz, *The Euro and its Threat to the Future of Europe* (London, Penguin, 2017), p. 5.

28. *Nouvel Observateur*, 31 Dec. 1998, p. 22.

29. Moore, *Margaret Thatcher*, vol. III, p. 645.

30. Hansard House of Commons debates, 13 Nov. 1990, vol. 180, cols. 461–5.

31. Mody, *EuroTragedy*, p. 93.

32. The Maastricht Treaty (formally known as the Treaty on European Union) came into force on 1 November 1993, inaugurating a new European Union, with the EEC as one of its 'pillars'.

33. Brendan Simms, *Unfinest Hour: Britain and the Destruction of Bosnia* (London, Penguin, 2003), p. 111.

34. Douglas Hurd, *Memoirs* (London, Little, Brown, 2003), p. 471.

35. *L'Événement du Jeudi*, 24 Sept. 1992, p. 10.

36. *Guardian*, 20 May 1993.

37. Mody, *EuroTragedy*, p. 93.

38. Ibid., pp. 97–8.

39. Eatwell and Goodwin, *National Populism*, p. 100.

40. BBC News, 25 June 1998.

41. Jon Davis and John Rentoul, *Heroes or Villains? The Blair Government Reconsidered* (Oxford, Oxford University Press, 2019), p. 217.

42. Gillingham, *European Integration*, p. 340.

43. 'Labour mobility within the EU', Discussion Paper 379, National Institute of Economic and Social Research, April 2011; ONS, 'Population by country of birth and nationality report, August 2013', fig. 5.

44. *The Economist*, 3 Nov. 2007, p. 33.

45. Ray Bassett, *Ireland and the EU Post Brexit* (Dublin, Grangeland Ventures, 2020), p. 224.

46. Tony Blair, *A Journey* (London, Hutchinson, 2010), p. 531.

47. Helen Thompson, 'Inevitability and contingency: the political economy of Brexit', *British Journal of Politics and International Relations* 19, 3 (2017), pp. 434–49.

48. Simon Jenkins, in the *Sunday Times*, 5 June 2005.

49. Anthony Barnett, *The Lure of Greatness: England's Brexit and America's Trump* (London, Unbound, 2017), p. 266.

50. Harold D. Clarke, Matthew Goodwin and Paul Whiteley, *Brexit: Why Britain Voted to Leave the European Union* (Cambridge, Cambridge University Press, 2017), pp. 188–90.

51. This is devastatingly analysed by Stiglitz, *The Euro*, and Mody, *EuroTragedy*.

52. Alessandro Gasparotti and Matthias Kullas, '20 years of the Euro: winners and losers', Centre for European Policy, Feb. 2019, https://www.cep.eu/Studien/20_Jahre_Euro_-_Gewinner_und_Verlierer/cepStudy_20_years_Euro_-_Winners_and_Losers.pdf.

53. https://www.reuters.com/article/germany-economy-trade/germany-to-run-worlds-largest-current-account-surplus-in-2019-ifo-idUSL5N2641DF.

54. Stefan Kawalec, 'The permanent necessity to undervalue the euro endangers Europe's trade relations', 12th EURO-FRAME Conference on Economic Policy Issues in the European Union, June 2015, https://www.euroframe.org/files/user_upload/euroframe/docs/2015/conference/Session%203/EUROF15_Kawalec.pdf.

55. Markus K. Brunnermeier, Harold James and Jean-Pierre Landau, *The Euro and the Battle of Ideas* (Princeton, NJ, Princeton University Press, 2016).

56. UK exports to non-EU destinations have grown by around 3.5% per year since 1998 (almost four times faster than exports to the EU) and 3.3% per year since 2007 (thirteen times faster): https://briefingsforbritain.co.uk/the-eu-is-a-major-drag-on-the-uk-economy/.

57. Barnabas Reynolds, David Blake and Robert Lyddon, 'Managing Euro risk', Politeia, 27 Feb. 2020, https://www.politeia.co.uk/managing-euro-risk-saving-investors-from-systemic-risk-by-barnabas-reynolds-david-blake-and-robert-lyddon/.

58. Andrew Rawnsley, *The End of the Party* (London, Viking, 2010), p. 581.

59. Mody, *EuroTragedy*, p. 204.

60. See Perry Anderson, 'The Italian disaster', *London Review of Books* 36, 10, 22 May 2014, pp. 3–16; and Yanis Varoufakis, *Adults in the Room: My Battle with Europe's Deep Establishment* (London, Vintage, 2018).

61. For a statement of the problem, see Stiglitz, *The Euro*; and for a concise explanation of why it cannot be solved, Paul Collier, 'Euro septic', *TLS*, 30 Sept. 2016.

62. Clarke, Goodwin and Whiteley, *Brexit*, p. 5.

63. Thompson, 'Inevitability and contingency', p. 17.

64. See Tim Shipman, *All Out War: The Full Story of Brexit* (London, William Collins, 2017), pp. 3–11.

65. José Ignacio Torreblanca et al., 'The continent-wide rise of Euroscepticism', European Council on Foreign Relations, May 2013, p. 1. For a fuller analysis of the roots of Euroscepticism, see Peter Mair, *Ruling the Void: The Hollowing of Western Democracy* (London, Verso, 2013), ch. 4. For statistics, see Clarke, Goodwin and Whiteley, *Brexit*, pp. 217–19.

66. Standard Eurobarometer 79 (Spring 2013).

67. John Curtice, 'How deeply does Britain's Euroscepticism run?', National Centre for Social Research, 2016.

68. Thompson, 'Inevitability and contingency', pp. 17–18.

69. Shipman, *All Out War*, p. 189.

70. This is argued in different ways by Brendan Simms, *Britain's Europe: A Thousand Years of Conflict and Cooperation* (London, Penguin, 2017) and Stuart Sweeney, *The Europe Illusion: Britain, France, Germany and the Long History of European Integration* (London, Reaktion, 2019).

71. An exhaustive and lively narrative is Shipman, *All Out War*.

72. Dominic Cummings, 'How the Brexit referendum was won', *Spectator*, 9 Jan. 2017.

73. See *Guardian*, 21 and 23 Nov. 2016.

74. Electoral Commission results, https://www.electoralcommission.org.uk/who-we-are-and-what-we-do/elections-and-referendums/past-elections-and-referendums/eu-referendum/results-and-turnout-eu-referendum.

4. DIVISIONS AND IDENTITIES

1. *Guardian*, 12 May 2017.

2. *Guardian*, Jan. 2018, quoted in Roger Eatwell and Matthew Goodwin, *National Populism: The Revolt against Liberal Democracy* (London, Penguin, 2018), p. 105.

3. Philip Cunliffe, *The New Twenty Years' Crisis: A Critique of International Relations, 1999–2019* (London, McGill-Queen's University Press, 2020), p. 115.

4. The best account is Tim Shipman, *All Out War: The Full Story of Brexit* (London, William Collins, 2017), pp. 530–45.

5. All statistics are taken from the Electoral Commission report.

6. David Goodhart, *The Road to Somewhere: The Populist Revolt and the Future of Politics* (London, Hurst, 2017), p. 19.

7. Eatwell and Goodwin, *National Populism*, p. 104.

8. Stephen Davies, *The Economics and Politics of Brexit: The Realignment of British Public Life* (Great Barrington, MA, American Institute for Economic Research, 2020), p. 101.

9. Mary Harrington, 'Pity the poor avocado-eating graduates', UnHerd, 11 Nov. 2019, https://unherd.com/2019/11/young-urban-graduates-the-real-left-behinds/.

10. *The Times*, 14 Dec. 2019.

11. Sir Paul Collier, 'Achieving socio-economic convergence in Europe', *Intereconomics* 55, 1 (2020), pp. 5–12.

12. Ipsos-MORI, 'How Britain voted in the 2016 EU referendum', 2016, https://www.ipsos.com/ipsos-mori/en-uk/how-britain-voted-2016-eu-referendum.

13. B. Pawlowski et al., 'Sex differences in everyday risk-taking behavior in humans', *Evolutionary Psychology* 6, 1 (2008), pp. 29–42.

14. Eurobarometer polls showed nothing like 60 per cent approval for the EU across Europe.

15. *Irish Times*, 28 Jan. 2016.

16. 'Euroskepticism beyond Brexit', Pew Research Center, 7 June 2016.

17. Ashoka Mody, *EuroTragedy: A Drama in Nine Acts* (Oxford, Oxford University Press, 2018), pp. 188–9, 404.

18. 'What Europe means to the young', *The Economist*, 5 Sept. 2015.

19. UNESCO, 'Global flow of tertiary-level students', 2020, http://uis.unesco.org/en/uis-student-flow; European Commission, 'United Kingdom: Erasmus+ 2018 in numbers', https://ec.europa.eu/programmes/erasmus-plus/resources/documents/united-kingdom-erasmus-2018-numbers_en.

20. On the social effects of universities, see Goodhart, *Road to Somewhere*, pp. 33–8; on social media, see Shoshana Zuboff, *The Age of Surveillance Capitalism: The Fight for a Human Future at the New Frontier of Power* (London, Profile, 2019), ch. 16.

21. Roberto Stefan Foa and Yascha Mounk, 'The danger of deconsolidation: the democratic disconnect', *Journal of Democracy* 27, 3, 2016, pp. 5–17.

22. Hugo Young, *This Blessed Plot: Britain and Europe from Churchill to Blair* (London, Macmillan, 1998), p. 507.

23. Lord Ashcroft poll, https://lordashcroftpolls.com/2016/06/how-the-united-kingdom-voted-and-why/.

24. Neema Begum, 'Minority ethnic attitudes and the 2016 EU referendum', Brexit and Public Opinion (UK in a Changing Europe), https://ukandeu.ac.uk/wp-content/uploads/2018/01/Public-Opinion.pdf.

25. Ben Cobley, *The Tribe: The Liberal-Left and the System of Diversity* (Exeter, Imprint Academic, 2018), ch. 4.

26. See, for example, European Agency for Fundamental Human Rights, 'Being Black in the EU: second European Union minorities and discrimination survey summary'. Countries with the worst records include Finland, Austria, Ireland and Denmark.

27. 'Euroskepticism beyond Brexit', Pew Research Center.

28. Richard Tuck, *The Left Case for Brexit* (Cambridge, Polity Press, 2020), p. 147.

29. 'How many Labour supporters voted Leave?', Reality Check, BBC News, 29 Apr. 2019.

30. 'Euroskepticism beyond Brexit', Pew Research Center; Eurobarometer polls give a similar picture.

31. *Le Monde*, 12 Mar. 2016.

32. *The Andrew Marr Show*, BBC 1, 21 Jan. 2018.

33. Institut Montaigne, 'Les Français et l'Union européenne', 4 Oct. 2018.

34. Mody, *EuroTragedy*, pp. 421–4.

35. 'Seven days to save the EU', European Council on Foreign Relations, 16 May 2019, https://www.ecfr.eu/article/commen tary_seven_days_to_save_the_european_union.

36. John Curtice, 'How deeply does Britain's Euroscepticism run?', National Centre for Social Research, 2016, pp. 6–8.

37. Alain Peyrefitte, *C'était de Gaulle* (Paris, Fayard, 1994), vol. I, p. 63.

38. David Reynolds, *Island Stories: Britain and its History in the Age of Brexit* (London, William Collins, 2019), p. 91.

39. Eurobarometer, July 2013.

40. Ian Kershaw, *To Hell and Back: Europe 1914–1949* (London, Penguin, 2016), pp. 518–22.

41. Justyna Salamońska and Ettore Recchi, 'Europe between mobility and sedentarism: patterns of cross-border practices

and their consequences for European identification', EU Working Paper RSCAS 2016/50, European University Institute, Robert Schuman Centre for Advanced Studies, Migration Policy Centre, 2016.

42. Goodhart, *Road to Somewhere*, p. 104.

43. For a reasoned statement of this view by a constitutional lawyer, see Richard Ekins, 'Constitutional conversations in Britain (in Europe)', in G. Sigalet, G. Webber and R. Dixon, eds., *Constitutional Dialogue: Rights, Democracy, Institutions* (Cambridge, Cambridge University Press, 2019), pp. 436–65.

44. See Davies, *The Economics and Politics of Brexit*.

45. Lord Ashcroft Poll – a large exit poll on the day of the vote.

46. Ibid.

47. Cris Shore, *Building Europe: The Cultural Politics of European Integration* (London, Routledge, 2000), p. 207.

48. Tony Judt, *A Grand Illusion? An Essay on Europe* (London, Penguin, 1997), p. 4.

49. John Gray, 'Brexit has left the British political class trapped by its own history', *New Statesman*, 13 Mar. 2019.

50. In the 2014 referendum, 1,617,989 had voted for Scottish independence.

51. George Orwell, *Essays* (Penguin Classics, 2000), p. 156.

52. In a public debate at Hughes Hall, Cambridge, in June 2016 in which he and I were speakers. I quote from memory.

53. *Sunday Times*, 5 June 2005.

54. Peter Mair, *Ruling the Void: The Hollowing of Western Democracy* (London, Verso, 2013), pp. 75–6, 99.

55. Nick Busvine, 'Is the civil service impartial?', 10 Aug. 2019, https://briefingsforbritain.co.uk/is-the-civil-service-impartial.

56. Dominic Cummings, 'How the Brexit referendum was won', *Spectator*, 9 Jan. 2017.

57. Standard Eurobarometer 79, Spring 2013, QA3a.2 and QA11a.2.

58. E.g. William Waldegrave, *Three Circles into One* (London, Mensch Publishing, 2019).

59. Collier, 'Achieving socio-economic convergence in Europe', p. 8.

60. Gray, 'Brexit has left the British political class trapped by its own history'.

61. Harold D. Clarke, Matthew Goodwin and Paul Whiteley, *Brexit: Why Britain Voted to Leave the European Union* (Cambridge, Cambridge University Press, 2017), p. 148.

62. Goodhart, *Road to Somewhere*, p. 119.

63. See Clarke, Goodwin and Whiteley, *Brexit*, pp. 99–103, 153–70; Goodhart, *Road to Somewhere*, pp. 20, 56–64, 119–22.

64. Goodhart, *Road to Somewhere*, p. 118.

65. See Clarke, Goodwin and Whiteley, *Brexit*, p. 157, and Goodhart, *Road to Somewhere*, pp. 8, 26–7.

66. Cummings, 'How the Brexit referendum was won'. Those interested in the gory details cannot do better than Shipman, *All Out War*.

67. Eurobarometer 79, Spring 2013, QA22a.9 (p. T97).

68. Shipman, *All Out War*, pp. 189–94.

69. Curtice, 'How deeply does Britain's Euroscepticism run?'; Clarke, Goodwin and Whiteley, *Brexit*, pp. 33–5.

70. For details, Shipman, *All Out War*, pp. 189–94, 234–6.

71. A source close to Osborne, quoted by Shipman, ibid., p. 246.

72. Clarke, Goodwin and Whiteley, *Brexit*, pp. 33, 51.

73. For the only full analysis made, based on a million pieces of trade data, see K. Coutts, G. Gudgin and J. Buchanan, 'How the economics profession got it wrong on Brexit', Centre for Business Research, University of Cambridge, Working Paper No.

493, 2018, esp. pp. 14–15, 20–21; and G. Gudgin, K. Coutts, N. Gibson and J. Buchanan, 'The role of gravity models in estimating the economic impact of Brexit', Centre for Business Research, University of Cambridge, Working Paper No. 490, 2017.

74. https://assets.publishing.service.gov.uk/government/uploads/system/uploads/attachment_data/file/220968/foi_eumembership_trade.pdf: table on page 7.

75. 'HM Treasury analysis: the immediate economic impact of leaving the EU', Cm 9292, May 2016.

76. House of Commons, 15 June 2016.

77. https://briefingsforbritain.co.uk/customs-costs-post-brexit-long-version/.

78. Lord King on *Today*, BBC Radio 4, 29 Mar. 2019.

79. 'The macroeconomics of brexit: motivated reasoning?' *New York Times*, 30 June 2016.

80. *Independent*, 6 Dec. 2018.

81. 'Defying gravity: a critique of estimates of the economic impact of Brexit', Policy Exchange, 26 June 2017.

82. For a statistical summary, Clarke, Goodwin and Whitely, *Brexit*, pp. 187–90, and for detailed analysis see Coutts, Gudgin and Buchanan, 'How the economics profession got it wrong', pp. 3–7.

83. https://briefingsforbritain.co.uk/the-eu-has-hardly-covered-itself-in-glory-with-brexit/.

84. *Independent*, 6 Dec. 2018.

85. Davies, *The Economics and Politics of Brexit*, p. 188.

86. Ibid., p. 103.

87. John Lloyd, *Should Auld Acquaintance Be Forgot: The Great Mistake of Scottish Independence* (Cambridge, Polity Press, 2020), pp. 50–51.

88. Curtice, 'How deeply does Britain's Euroscepticism run?', p. 7; Lloyd, *Auld Acquaintance*, pp. 8, 25.

89. Lloyd, *Auld Acquaintance*, p. 11.

90. Goodhart, *Road to Somewhere*, pp. 134–45; *The Economist*, 23 May 2020.

91. Timothy Garton Ash in the *Guardian*, 10 Sept. 2019.

92. A data company accused of manipulating public opinion, but which the Information Commission found in October 2020 had taken no part in the referendum campaign.

93. Timothy Garton Ash in the *Guardian*, 14 Dec. 2019.

94. Sir Vince Cable, Liberal Democrat leader, speech at party conference, 11 Mar. 2018.

95. One of the liveliest, best informed, and most alarmist was Ian Dunt, *Brexit: What the Hell Happens Now?* (Kingston upon Thames, Canbury Press, 2016).

96. Davies, *The Economics and Politics of Brexit*, pp. 110–11.

97. Waldegrave, *Three Circles*, p. 36.

98. Simon Kuper, *Financial Times*, 2 Nov. 2017.

99. Fintan O'Toole, *Heroic Failure: Brexit and the Politics of Pain* (London, Head of Zeus, 2019).

100. Robert Gildea, *Empires of the Mind: The Colonial Past and the Politics of the Present* (Cambridge, Cambridge University Press, 2019), p. 260; Garton Ash in the *Guardian*, 14 Dec. 2019.

101. Danny Dorling and Sally Tomlinson, *Rule Britannia: Brexit and the End of Empire* (London, Biteback Publishing, 2019).

102. Gray, 'Brexit has left the British political class trapped by its own history'.

103. Tuck, *The Left Case for Brexit*, p. 145.

104. Cobley, *The Tribe*, pp. 17–19.

105. *Guardian*, 8 Sept. 2017.

106. David Keighley and Andrew Jubb, *The Brussels Broadcasting Corporation? How Pro-Brexit Views Have Been Marginalised in the BBC's News Coverage* (London, Civitas, 2018), p. 43.

107. https://briefingsforbritain.co.uk/looking-beyond-brexit-a-view-from-australia-by-the-hon-john-howard/.

108. *Times Higher Education*, 16 June 2016.

109. J. D. Taylor, *Island Story: Journeys Through Unfamiliar Britain* (London, Repeater Books, 2016).

110. James Meek, *Dreams of Leaving and Remaining* (London, Verso, 2019), p. 104.

111. Ibid., p. 6.

112. Anthony Barnett, *The Lure of Greatness: England's Brexit and America's Trump* (London, Unbound, 2017).

113. In the *Guardian*, 20 March, 9 April, 10 September, 14 December 2019.

114. See 'Brexit and science funding: what exactly is the problem?', Briefings for Brexit, 30 Oct. 2018, https://briefingsforbritain.co.uk/brexit-and-science-funding-what-exactly-is-the-problem/.

115. Perry Anderson, in *New Left Review* 125, Sept.–Oct. 2020.

116. Several young academics brave enough to support Leave openly wrote on websites such as The Full Brexit and Briefings for Brexit (with which I was associated); we advised those without secure positions not to use their names.

117. Reynolds, *Island Stories*; Brendan Simms, *Britain's Europe: A Thousand Years of Conflict and Cooperation* (London, Penguin, 2017); Stuart Sweeney, *The Europe Illusion: Britain, France, Germany and the Long History of European Integration* (London, Reaktion, 2019).

118. Jürgen Osterhammel, *The Transformation of the World: A Global History of the Nineteenth Century* (Princeton, NJ, Princeton University Press, 2014), p. 456.

119. Kevin O'Rourke, *A Short History of Brexit: From Brentry to Backstop* (London, Penguin, 2019).

120. Mody, *EuroTragedy*.

121. Roger Scruton, *Where We Are: The State of Britain Now* (London, Bloomsbury, 2017).

122. *New Statesman*, 8 May 2017.

123. Tuck, *The Left Case for Brexit*; Graham Gudgin, Briefings for Brexit, *passim*.

124. Eatwell and Goodwin, *National Populism*.

125. Chris Bickerton, *The European Union: A Citizen's Guide* (London, Penguin, 2016).

126. Vernon Bogdanor, *Beyond Brexit: Towards a British Constitution* (London, I. B. Tauris, 2019).

127. Paul Collier, 'Getting somewhere', *Prospect*, Aug.–Sept. 2020; and see Paul Collier and John Kay, *Greed is Dead: Politics after Individualism* (London, Allen Lane, 2020).

128. Davies, *The Economics and Politics of Brexit*.

129. Goodhart, *Road to Somewhere*.

130. *Guardian*, 14 Dec. 2019.

131. Goodhart's categories, *Road to Somewhere*, pp. 44–7.

132. *Times Literary Supplement*, 30 Sept. 2016, p. 13.

5. STOPPING BREXIT — ALMOST

1. James Meek, *Dreams of Leaving and Remaining* (London, Verso, 2019), p. 1.

2. Thomas Hobbes, *Leviathan*, ed. Richard Tuck (Cambridge, Cambridge University Press, 2008), p. 231.

3. For example, in his speech on the future of Europe at the Sorbonne, 26 Sept. 2017.

4. Or cede it *back* to the EU, if one accepts the argument that Parliament had abrogated its sovereignty by the European Communities Act (1972). See, e. g., Vernon Bogdanor, *Beyond*

Brexit: Towards a British Constitution (London, I. B. Tauris, 2019), p. 277.

5. Roger Scruton, *Where We Are: The State of Britain Now* (London, Bloomsbury, 2017), p. 23.

6. Tim Shipman, *Fall Out: A Year of Political Mayhem* (London, William Collins, 2018), p. 84.

7. Stephen Davies, *The Economics and Politics of Brexit: The Realignment of British Public Life* (Great Barrington, MA, American Institute for Economic Research, 2020), p. 133.

8. *Guardian*, 26 Nov. 2018.

9. Arguing that the judgment was legally weak are Richard Ekins and Graham Gee, 'Miller, constitutional realism and the politics of Brexit', in M. Elliott, J. Williams and A. L. Young, eds., *The UK Constitution after Miller: Brexit and Beyond* (Oxford, Hart Publishing, 2018), pp. 249–75.

10. Harold D. Clarke, Matthew Goodwin and Paul Whiteley, *Brexit: Why Britain Voted to Leave the European Union* (Cambridge, Cambridge University Press, 2017), p. 227.

11. BBC News, 22 June 2016.

12. *Spectator*, 4 July 2020.

13. Lord Kerr of Kinlochard (former diplomatic representative at the EU), Hansard House of Lords debates, 16 Jan. 2018, vol. 788, col. 585.

14. Garton Ash in the *Guardian*, 9 Apr. 2019.

15. James Rogers, ed., *Audit of Global Capability: An Assessment of Twenty Major Powers* (London, Henry Jackson Society, 2019).

16. Gabriel Felbermayr, 'Brexit: a hard-but-smart strategy and its consequences', *Intereconomics* 54, 3 (2019), pp. 178–83, https://www.intereconomics.eu/contents/year/2019/number/3/article/brexit-a-hard-but-smart-strategy-and-its-consequences.html.

17. 'Le chiffre du commerce extérieure', 2019–20, http://leki osque.finances.gouv.fr/; World Integrated Trade Solution statistics, https://wits.worldbank.org/CountryProfile/en/ Country/DEU/Year/2017/TradeFlow/EXPIMP/Partner/ by-country.

18. *Die Welt*, 10 Feb. 2019, https://www.welt.de/wirtschaft/ article188506313/Brexit-100-000-Jobs-in-Deutschland-bei-hartem-Ausstieg-in-Gefahr.html.

19. Felbermayr, 'Brexit'.

20. 'The withdrawal of the UK from the European Union', The Conservative European Research Group and Lawyers for Britain, Sept. 2017.

21. *Prospect* Magazine, June 2020.

22. Shipman, *Fall Out*, p. 81.

23. Manfred Weber, MEP, in *Irish Times*, 10 May 2017.

24. *Independent*, 30 May 2018.

25. 'The money behind Remain', Briefings for Brexit, 25 Mar. 2019, https://briefingsforbritain.co.uk/the-money-behind-remain/.

26. See Alan Halsall in *Sunday Telegraph*, 28 June 2020, p. 15.

27. See *Financial Times*, 25 June 2018.

28. Interview in *The Times*, 24 Mar. 2018.

29. Paul Collier, 'Capitalism after coronavirus', *New Statesman*, 8 May 2020.

30. Richard Johnson, 'The keys to Downing Street: leave-voting marginals', Briefings for Brexit, 11 Feb. 2019, https:// briefingsforbritain.co.uk/the-keys-to-downing-street-leave-voting-marginals/.

31. The ERG was founded in 1993; leading members included Bill Cash, Jacob Rees-Mogg, Steve Baker, Iain Duncan Smith, Suella Braverman, Owen Paterson, David Jones and Mark Francois.

32. Martin Howe QC, 'Legal advice to the Cabinet', Briefings for Brexit, 13 Nov. 2018, https://briefingsforbritain.co.uk/legal-advice-to-the-cabinet/.

33. E.g. Graham Gudgin and Ray Bassett, 'Getting over the line: solutions to the Irish border', Policy Exchange, 2018; 'Alternative arrangements for the Irish border: interim report 24th June 2019', Prosperity UK.

34. Lars Karlsson, 'Smart border 2.0: avoiding a hard border on the island of Ireland for Customs control and the free movement of persons', Nov. 2017, https://www.europarl.europa.eu/RegData/etudes/STUD/2017/596828/IPOL_STU(2017)596828_EN.pdf.

35. Ray Bassett, *Ireland and the EU Post Brexit* (Dublin, Grangeland Ventures, 2020), p. 26.

36. Ibid., p. 34.

37. Joseph E. Stiglitz, *The Euro and its Threat to the Future of Europe* (London, Penguin, 2016), pp. xxiii, 231.

38. John Fitzgerald and Edgar Morgenroth, 'The Northern Ireland economy: problems and prospects', Trinity College Dublin, TEP Working Paper No. 0619, July 2019, pp. 23–4, 33–6, https://econpapers.repec.org/paper/tcdtcduee/tep0619.htm.

39. David Jones MP, Hansard House of Commons debates, 6 Dec. 2018, vol. 650, col. 1134.

40. Howe, 'Legal advice to the Cabinet'.

41. For detailed analysis of votes and tactics, see Davies, *Economics and Politics of Brexit*, ch. 5.

42. Officially the European Union (Withdrawal) (No. 5) Bill.

43. Davies, *Economics and Politics of Brexit*, p. 205.

44. A. V. Dicey (1885), discussed in Colin Turpin and Adam Tomkins, *British Government and the Constitution* (Cambridge, Cambridge University Press, 2012), pp. 58–96.

45. Lord Steyn (2005), ibid., p. 78.

46. Richard Ekins and Sir Stephen Laws, 'Securing electoral accountability', Policy Exchange, 2019, p. 6. I am grateful to Richard Ekins, Professor of Law and Constitutional Government in the University of Oxford, for discussing these matters with me.

47. Officially the European Union (Withdrawal) (No. 2) Act 2019.

48. Garton Ash in the *Guardian*, 10 Sept. 2019.

49. Judgment of the Divisional Court (Case No: CO/3385/2019), 11 Sept. 2019, paras 63 and 68, https://www.judiciary.uk/wp-content/uploads/2019/09/Miller-No-FINAL-1.pdf.

50. John Finnis, 'The unconstitutionality of the Supreme Court's prorogation judgment', Policy Exchange, 2019, pp. 5, 18, 11.

51. Ibid., pp. 5, 10.

52. Reported by Charles Moore, *Daily Telegraph*, 25 July 2020.

53. For the unsavoury details, 'How the People's Vote fell apart', *Financial Times*, 7 Aug. 2020.

54. Johnson, 'The keys to Downing Street: leave-voting marginals'.

55. *The Times*, 14 Dec. 2019.

56. Davies, *Economics and Politics of Brexit*, pp. 227–39.

57. Details in Martin Howe QC, 'This flawed deal is a tolerable price to pay for our freedom,' Briefings for Brexit, 21 Oct. 2019, https://briefingsforbritain.co.uk/this-flawed-deal-is-a-tolerable-price-to-pay-for-our-freedom/.

58. *Libération*, 30 Jan. 2019: *L'Express*, 19 Jan. 2019.

6. COVID AND AFTER

1. Karl Marx, *Der achtzehnte Brumaire des Louis Bonaparte* (1852) (my translation).

2. Patrick West, 'How closely linked are lockdown and Brexit?', *Spectator*, 10 Oct. 2020.

3. Paul Collier, 'The problem of modelling: public policy and the coronavirus', *TLS*, 24 Apr. 2020.

4. Marie Daouda, 'History will judge those who emerged from lockdown to fight the ghost of Cecil Rhodes', *Daily Telegraph*, 18 June 2020.

5. Paul Sheard, 'The economics of Covid 19', Woori Financial Research Institute, Aug. 2020.

6. Russell Napier, 'Is France too big to save?', Briefings for Britain,19Apr.2020,https://briefingsforbritain.co.uk/is-france-too-big-to-save-the-debt-crisis-in-the-eu/.

7. *Guardian*, 11 Apr. 2020.

8. Bruegel Datasets: 'The fiscal response to the economic fallout from the coronavirus', 5 Aug. 2020; Ambrose Evans-Pritchard in the *Daily Telegraph*, 21 and 22 July and 3 Oct. 2020; Institute for Fiscal Studies, 'How does the size of the UK's fiscal response to coronavirus compare with other countries'?', 14 May 2020.

9. *Le Monde*, 11 May and 25 June 2020.

10. Joseph E. Stiglitz, *The Euro and its Threat to the Future of Europe* (London, Penguin, 2016), p. xxv.

11. 'Germany–Europe–Asia: shaping the 21st century together', https://www.auswaertiges-amt.de/blob/2380514/f9784f7e3b3 fa1bd7c5446d274a4169e/200901-indo-pazifik-leitlinien--1--data.pdf.

12. Institute for Fiscal Studies, 'How does the size of the UK's fiscal response to coronavirus compare with other countries'?', 14 May 2020.

13. Robert Lee, 'The Covid doomsters are wrong: the UK is heading for recovery', Briefings for Britain, 17 Aug. 2020, https://briefingsforbritain.co.uk/the-covid-doomsters-are-wrong-the-uk-is-heading-for-recovery/.

14. Lloyds Banking Group, 'UK private sector recovery ahead of global trend', 20 Aug. 2020.

15. Julian Jessop, 'In the wake of the chancellor's latest announcements, we should be more ready to cheer good economic news', Politeia, 25 Sept. 2020, https://www.politeia.co.uk/in-the-wake-of-the-chancellors-latest-announcements-we-should-be-more-ready-to-cheer-good-economic-news-by-julian-jessop/.

16. See speech by the Bank's chief economist, Andy Haldane, 'Avoiding economic anxiety', 30 Sept. 2020, https://www.bankofengland.co.uk/speech/2020/andy-haldane-keynote-speaker-at-the-cheshire-and-warrington-lep-economic-summit-and-agm-2020.

17. B. R. Mitchell and Phyllis Deane, *Abstract of British Historical Statistics* (Cambridge, Cambridge University Press, 1962), pp. 366, 368, 402–3.

18. Speech at Université Libre de Bruxelles, 17 Feb. 2020.

19. Manfred Weber, MEP, leader of the European People's Party in the European Parliament, in *Irish Times*, 10 May 2017.

20. Michel Barnier, news conference, 24 Apr. 2020.

21. 'Remarques de Michel Barnier suite au septième round de négociations sur un futur partenariat entre l'Union européenne et le Royaume-Uni', European Commission, 21 Aug. 2020.

22. *Nouvel Observateur*, 30 Sept. 2020.

23. *Financial Times*, 25 Oct. 2020.

24. For a critical summary, see *The Times*, 'Covid revealed sickness at the heart of Britain', 14 Aug. 2020.

25. See *Guardian*, 30 May 2019.

26. According to the Chinese Global Financial Centres Index, *Business Insider*, 25 Sept. 2020.

27. Chris Bickerton, *The European Union: A Citizen's Guide* (London, Penguin, 2016), p. 213. Ch. 6 is an excellent summary.

28. Tony Corn, '*Finis Austriae, Finis Europae?* L'Europe post-Brexit et le syndrome austro-hongrois', Academia, 2020, p. 8, https://www.academia.edu/42681691/Finis_Austriae_ Finis_Europae_LEurope_post_Brexit_et_le_syndrome_ austro_hongrois.

29. 'Angst in the Aegean', *The Economist*, 22 Aug. 2020.

30. A. Wess Mitchell, 'Perhapsburg: today's European Union is yesterday's Austro-Hungarian Empire on the gameboard of world politics', *The American Interest* 4, 2, Nov. 2008.

31. *Guardian*, 22 Oct. 2020.

32. See Clive Hamilton and Mareike Ohlberg, *Hidden Hand: Exposing How the Chinese Communist Party is Reshaping the World* (London, Oneworld Publications, 2020), pp. 56–67, 106–10, 133–8.

33. Erik Brattberg and Ben Judah, 'Forget the G-7, build the D-10', *Foreign Policy*, 10 June 2020.

CONCLUSION

1. Quoted by Tony Corn, '*Finis Austriae, Finis Europae?* L'Europe post-Brexit et le syndrome austro-hongrois', Academia, 2020, p. 14 (my translation), https://www.academia.edu/42681691/ Finis_Austriae_Finis_Europae_LEurope_post_Brexit_et_le_ syndrome_austro_hongrois.

2. Quoted in *Daily Telegraph*, 25 Mar. 2020.

3. Stephen Davies, *The Economics and Politics of Brexit: The Realignment of British Public Life* (Great Barrington, MA, American Institute for Economic Research, 2020), p. 236.

4. Michael Kenny and Nick Pearce, 'The empire strikes back', *New Statesman*, 23 Jan. 2017.

5. John Gray, 'Why this crisis is a turning point in history', *New Statesman*, 1 Apr. 2020.

6. *Guardian*, 26 Aug. 2020.

7. Neal Ascherson, 'Bye bye Britain', *London Review of Books*, 24 Sept. 2020, p. 37.

8. YouGov, 'What should the EU be?', 3 Aug. 2020.

9. See Macron's Sorbonne speech on the future of Europe, 26 Sept. 2017.

10. Tony Judt, *A Grand Illusion? An Essay on Europe* (London, Penguin, 1997), p. 3 – a penetrating essay still well worth reading.

11. Hugo Young, *This Blessed Plot: Britain and Europe from Churchill to Blair* (London, Macmillan, 1998), p. 510.

12. Judt, *Grand Illusion?*, p. 3.

13. Garton Ash in the *Guardian*, 20 Mar. 2019.

14. Yanis Varoufakis, *And the Weak Suffer What They Must? Europe, Austerity and the Threat to Global Stability* (London, Vintage, 2017).

15. Sir Paul Collier, 'Achieving socio-economic convergence in Europe', *Intereconomics* 55, 1 (2020), p. 8.

16. A classic analysis is Peter Mair, *Ruling the Void: The Hollowing of Western Democracy* (London, Verso, 2013), and, focusing on the EU, Christopher Bickerton, *European Integration: From Nation-States to Member States* (Oxford, Oxford University Press, 2012). On secrecy, see Yanis Varoufakis,

Adults in the Room: My Battle with Europe's Deep Establishment (London, Vintage, 2018), pp. 231–47.

17. At the Liberal Democrat conference at Bournemouth in September 2019. He was cheered.

18. Gray, 'Why this crisis is a turning point in history'.

19. William Waldegrave, *Three Circles into One* (London, Mensch Publishing, 2019), p. 113.

20. A perceptive if sceptical summary is by Michael Kenny and Nick Pearce, 'The rise of the Anglosphere: how the Right dreamed up a new conservative world order', *New Statesman*, 10 Feb. 2015.

21. 'Déclaration sur la politique de la mer', Montpellier, 3 Dec. 2019 (my translation). I am grateful to Tony Corn for this reference.

22. Csaba Barnabas Horvath, 'Global impacts of Brexit: a butterfly effect', *Eurasia Review*, 29 Feb. 2020.

Index

Acheson, Dean 29
Adenauer, Konrad 26
Adonis, Andrew 102
Æthelstan, king 3
Alcuin of York 3
Alfred 'the Great' 3
Allen, Heidi 82
Anglo-Saxons 2, 3, 4
Anglosphere 20, 64, 160–61
Anne, queen 7
Arrow, Kenneth viii
Asquith, H. H. 14
Atkinson, Kate 93
Augustine, saint 3
Australia 12, 90, 128, 140,
   147, 148–9, 161
Azeglio, Massimo d' 39, 157
   quoted 70

Baker, Steve 108, 186n31
Balls, Ed 48
Bank of England 53
Barnes, Julian 93
Barnett, Anthony 91
Barnier, Michel 93, 105,
   139, 142
BBC 88, 89–90, 107, 152
Bede, venerable 2, 3
Belgium 13, 15, 26

Benn, Hilary 116; 'Benn
   Act' 119, 121
Benn, Tony 37
Bercow, John 114, 116
Best for Britain 106–7
Bevin, Ernest 23, 24
Bickerton, Christopher
   vii, 94
Biden, Joe 142
Bill of Rights (1689) 8, 120
Bismarck, Otto von 14
Blair, Tony 47–50, 101, 107
Boadicea, queen 1
Bogdanor, Vernon 94
Bombay 8
Brexit Party 71, 107, 115,
   121, 122–3
Briefings for Brexit viii,
   183n116
Brown, Gordon 48
Burchill, Julie 93
Burke, Edmund 100
Busvine, Nick 74
Bute, 3rd earl of 1

Caesar, Julius 1
Cambridge Analytica 87
Cambridge, University of
   73, 92

Cameron, David vii, 15,
55–8, 60, 68, 79, 90,
100
Campbell, Alistair 101
Canada 9
Castlereagh, Viscount 13
Chamberlain, Joseph 12, 159
Charlemagne 3
Charles II 8, 147
Chaucer, Geoffrey 5
Chequers White Paper (July
2018) 108
China 14, 22, 103, 110, 126,
128, 146–8, 159, 162
and UK 146–9
chlorinated chicken 140
Christianity 1, 2, 3
Churchill, Winston 9, 16,
24, 131, 146
City of London 8, 53,
104, 144
Clarke, Ken 109
Clegg, Nick 108
Coe, Jonathan 93
Cold War 18, 20, 23, 64
Collier, Paul 62, 94,
96, 157
Common Agricultural
Policy 31, 35, 36,
common currency 23
see also Euro currency
Common Fisheries Policy
33, 111, 138–9
Common Law 4, 70, 100
Common Market 13, 23, 32

Commonwealth 20, 23, 24,
25, 26, 27, 29, 30, 31,
32, 35–7, 69, 147, 162
Confederation of British
Industry 47, 82, 107
Conservative Party 41, 43,
71, 106, 108–9, 115–16,
122–3, 152
Constitution, UK 102
challenge to 114–21, 154
see also Fixed-term
Parliaments Act (2011);
Parliament, United
Kingdom; royal
prerogative; sovereignty;
Supreme Court
Corbyn, Jeremy 105, 109,
110, 122
Court of Session, Scotland
119
COVID-19 126–33, 138, 142
aftermath 143–4, 147, 153
Cox, Jo 58
Cromwell, Oliver 7
Cummings, Dominic 74,
123, 127–8, 142

Davies, Stephen 94
Davis, David 104–5, 108
Delors, Jacques 38–43, 157
Delors Plan 42–3
democratic deficit 40, 157–8
Democratic Unionist Party
(DUP) 106, 111
Denmark 34

Disraeli, Benjamin 14
Divisional Court, England
    101, 119

Economic and Monetary
    Union (EMU) 33, 38,
    42, 46
Economist, The 90
Edward (the Elder), king 3
Edward the Confessor 3
Edward III 5
Electoral Commission 107, 152
Elizabeth I, queen 6, 19
Elizabeth II, queen 127, 162
Empire, British 9, 10, 11, 12,
    13, 17-18, 20, 23, 30
England 3, 4, 5, 6, 73, 122, 154
    English language 4,
    9-10, 12
    English literature 9
    Englishness 86-8, 95
Euro currency 42-3, 44,
    46-7, 50, 157
    Britain does not adopt 48
    Eurozone problems 50-54,
    70, 126, 132-6, 142-3
European Central Bank
    (ECB) 42, 44, 53, 54,
    135-6
European Coal and Steel
    Community 25, 79
European Commission
    38-9, 43, 108, 133
European Council of
    Ministers 38, 43, 134

European Court of Justice
    97, 110, 124, 135
European Customs Union
    97, 100, 108, 113
European Economic
    Community (EEC)
    26, 29
    British entry 29-34
European Free Trade
    Association (EFTA)
    32, 101
European Monetary System
    (EMS) 38, 42
European Parliament 43
    elections to: (2004) 49;
    (2009) 49; (2014)
    55-6; (2019) 115-16
European Research Group
    110, 113, 186n31
European supranationalism/
    integration 13, 15-16,
    19, 20, 23, 24, 25,
    39-40, 72, 154-7
    'magical thinking' 46_7
    see also Euro currency;
    Single European Market
European Union (EU) vii,
    18, 45
    economic growth 83-4, 132
    international weakness 145
    negotiations with UK
    104-5, 108-13, 138-42
    political void 157-9
    public opinion 54, 55-6,
    63-4, 66-7, 95, 155-6

Exchange Rate Mechanism
(ERM) 42–3, 45–6

Fairbairn, Carolyn 82
Farage, Nigel 49, 60, 78, 115
financial crisis (2007–8) 48,
52–5
Financial Times 90
Fixed-term Parliaments
Act (2011) 114, 116,
118, 125
Floyd, George 130
Fox, Liam 104
France 5, 7, 13, 14, 15, 16,
17, 31, 65–7, 70, 103–4,
125, 130, 132–3, 137,
145, 160, 161
British links with 5, 6,
10, 18
economic growth 28, 35
and European integration
25, 32, 42, 157
'Second Hundred Years
War' 8, 11
Franks 4
free trade 11–12, 30,
31–2, 150
Frost, David 138–9, 146

Garton Ash, Timothy 91, 95
Gaulle, Charles de vii, 32-3,
39, 68
General elections: (2017)
105–6; (2019) 122–4, 151
George I 7

Germany 1, 5, 10, 14, 15,
16–18, 23, 31–2, 36, 41,
65, 70, 103–4, 127, 128,
130, 134–6, 137, 161
and European integration
25–6, 41–2, 51–2,
68, 157
benefits from 50–51
Giscard d'Estaing, Valéry 44
Gladstone, W. E. 131
Global Britain 69, 148
Glorious Revolution (1688)
7, 100
Goodhart, David 77, 85, 95
Goodwin, Matthew 94
Gove, Michael 60, 78, 79,
87, 101, 110
Gray, John 72–3, 76, 88,
94, 153, 159
Great Reform Act (1832) 100
Greece 13, 46, 53–4, 63,
67–8, 99, 121, 145, 158
Green Party 65, 152
Grieve, Dominic 114, 116
Guardian 89, 90
Gudgin, Graham 94, 180n73

Hammond, Philip 82,
101, 105
Hanover 7, 18, 19
Harold, king 4
Hastings, battle 4
hate crime 89
Heath, Edward 33, 36
Henry V 5

Henry VIII 4, 5, 6
Heseltine, Michael 109
Hitler, Adolf 2, 16, 17, 19, 41
Hobbes, Thomas 98–9
Hollande, François 150
Holy Roman Empire 5,
    6, 21
Hong Kong 147
Howard, John 90
Howe, Geoffrey 41, 43–4
Hudgell, Tony 127
Hungary 1, 70, 142
Hurd, Douglas 45

identity, European 158
identity, national 158, 159
immigration to UK 48–9,
    54–5, 71, 77, 143, 149
India 8, 9, 149, 161, 162
Internal Market Bill (2020)
    140–41
invasions of British Isles 1,
    2, 3, 4, 6, 7, 10, 14
Ireland 4, 5, 6, 8, 15, 34,
    53–4, 63, 73, 99,
    111–12, 153, 154
  border issue 108, 111–12,
    124, 139, 140–41
  see also Northern Ireland
Italy 5, 10, 14, 17, 46, 53–4,
    66–8, 70, 99, 121, 126,
    130, 132–3, 135, 137,
    145, 158
  economic growth 2
    8, 135

James VI and I 7, 10
Japan 14, 17, 148, 149
Jenkins, Simon 73
Johnson, Boris 60, 78, 87,
    101, 107, 108, 116,
    118–21, 123–5, 129,
    138, 141, 143, 148
Jóźwik, Arkadiusz 89
Judt, Tony 42, 156
Juncker, Jean-Claude 47,
    50, 89, 97, 157

Kaldor, Nicholas 36
Kershaw, Ian 69
Keynes, J. M. 15
King, Mervyn 82–3
Kinnock, Neil 44, 49
Knut (Canute), king 3
Kohl, Helmut 41, 46, 157
Krugman, Paul 83
Kundera, Milan 156

Labour Party 33, 36, 41,
    44, 71, 105–6, 109,
    122–3, 152
Lamont, Norman 44
Laski, Harold 22
Lawson, Nigel 43
League of Nations 15, 72, 150
Letwin, Oliver 116
'level playing field'
    138–9, 142
Leyen, Ursula von der 125
Liberal Democrats 71, 97,
    101, 115, 122, 152

Liberal Party 150
London 61, 86, 116, 158
Louis XIV 7, 10, 147
Low Countries/Netherlands
6, 7, 8, 10, 18, 19, 26,
50–51, 63, 65, 66, 134

Macmillan, Harold 26,
30, 32
Macron, Emmanuel 63, 66,
99, 133, 155, 157, 161
Major, John 44, 45, 109, 117
Malcolm, Noel 91–2
Marx, Karl 126
Mary I, queen 6, 19
Mary II, queen 7
May, Theresa 79, 82, 93,
101, 102, 103, 104, 105,
108, 110, 111, 113, 114,
116, 124, 140
McEwan, Ian 60, 93
Meek, James 91, 97
Mendès-France, Pierre 22
Merkel, Angela 50,
126–7, 133
Michel, Charles 125
Miller, Gina 101, 106,
117, 119
Mitterrand, François 37, 39,
41–2, 157
Mody, Ashoka 67, 83, 85, 93
Monde, Le viii, 90
Monnet, Jean 25, 69, 157
Moore, 'Captain Tom' 127
Mosley, Oswald 16

Napoleon, emperor 9, 19, 49
NATO 37, 155
guarantor of peace in
Europe 145
Nelson, Horatio 2
New York Times 90
New Zealand 90, 128,
129, 147
Norman Conquest 2, 5
North America 9
see also United States of
America
Northern Ireland 62–3, 86,
124, 139
'backstop' protocol
111–13, 114, 118,
124, 141
Northumbria, kingdom 3
Norway 33, 100, 124

O'Neill, Con 22, 27,
29–30, 33
O'Rourke, Kevin 93
O'Toole, Fintan 87–8
Obama, Barack 79
Offa, king 3
Open Britain 101, 106, 122
Orwell, George 73
Osborne, George 79–80, 81
Oxford, University of 88

Paisley, Ian 37
Parliament, United Kingdom
70, 87, 102, 113–14,
124, 152

claim to sovereignty 99,
117
prorogation 116, 117,
119–20
see also general elections;
sovereignty
Peel, Robert 11, 131
Poland 1, 69, 70, 142
Political Declaration (PD)
110, 124, 140
Pompidou, Georges 33
Portugal 8, 68, 132, 158
Powell, Enoch 37
Project Fear 75, 78–85, 91, 96

Raab, Dominic 109
referendum on Scottish
independence (2014)
79, 100
referendums on Europe: 46,
49–50, 63, 66
on Maastricht Treaty in
France and Denmark
(1992) 45–7, 66
on Euro in Denmark
(2000) and Sweden
(2003) 47–8, 66
on European Constitution
in France and
Netherlands (2005)
49–50, 63, 66
in Ireland: (2001) 48;
(2008) 50
in Greece (2015) 63, 66
in Denmark (2015) 66

in Netherlands (2016) 66
in UK: (1975) vii, 36–7;
promised by Tony Blair
47; cancelled 50;
required by European
Union Act (2011) 55;
promised by David
Cameron (2013) 55; on
EU membership (2016)
57–9, 60–67, 71–85;
attempts to explain
85–96; demands for
second referendum 97,
106, 115, 118, 122
Reformation 6, 10
Reynolds, David 92
Robbins, Oliver 105
Rogers, Ivan 105
Roman empire 3
royal prerogative 101,
114, 119
Russia 13, 14, 17, 18, 31,
87, 147, 149, 160

Schuman, Robert 25, 157
Scotland 4, 5, 6, 8, 9, 10,
19, 62–3, 86, 129,
153–4
see also referendum on
Scottish independence
(2014)
Scottish National Party 63,
71, 73, 119, 122,
123, 153
Scruton, Roger 94, 100

sea power 2, 10–11, 14, 17, 19, 148–9
Shakespeare, William 2, 5, 9
Sheard, Paul 84
Simms, Brendan 92
Singapore 128, 159
Single European Market 38, 52, 97, 100, 108, 113
slavery 9, 13, 131
Smith, Ali 93
Soros, George 106–7
sovereignty 71, 85, 98–100, 101, 117–18, 184n4
Spain 8, 10, 13,19, 65–6, 68, 127, 130, 132–3, 137, 158
Spanish armada 6
Stability and Growth Pact 44
Stiglitz, Joseph 42, 136
Sturgeon, Nicola 93
Suez crisis (1956) 27, 31
Sunak, Rishi 136
Supreme Court 70, 101–2, 117, 119–20, 152
Sweden 66, 126, 129, 130
Sweeney, Stuart 92
Switzerland 159

Thatcher, Margaret 37–9, 40–41, 43–4
   Bruges speech 40–41
Tickell, Crispin 35
Times, The 89

Tories 8, 37
   see also Conservative Party
trade 10, 11–12, 13, 24, 31–2, 102–4, 140, 149
   see also free trade
Trans-Pacific Partnership 149
Treasury, UK 79, 80–82
Treaties
   Dunkirk (1947) 23
   Brussels (1948) 23
   North Atlantic (1949) 24
   Paris (1951) 25
   Rome (1957) 26, 32
   Maastricht (1992) 44–5
   Lisbon (2007) 50, 101, 104, 113, 118
Trump, Donald 90
Tuck, Richard 88, 94
Turkey 145
Turner, Janice 62, 123

United Kingdom 8, 10, 153
   contacts beyond Europe 11
   declinism 26–31, 33, 76
   economic growth 2 7–9, 33, 35–6, 52, 132, 137–8
   and the Euro 48, 52
   and European integration 24–7, 56–7, 58, 67–78
   leaves EU 125, 162
   member of EU 155–6
   negotiations with EU 104–5, 108–13, 138–42

peace in Europe 11,
13, 160
strategic choices 145–9,
160–62
trade with EU 52, 81, 83,
103–4, 174n56
see also Constitution, UK;
England; general
elections; Northern
Ireland; referendums on
Europe; Scotland;
sovereignty; Wales
United Kingdom
Independence Party
(UKIP) 49, 54, 55-6,
71, 77
see also Brexit Party
United Nations 37, 72
United States of America 9,
12, 17–18, 20, 24, 29,
32, 69, 79, 90, 127,
128, 130, 146, 161
universities 91–2
see also Cambridge,
University of; Oxford,
University of

Varadkar, Leo 93
Varoufakis, Yanis 150, 151
Védrine, Hubert 35
Verhofstadt, Guy 159
vocational training 143–4

Waldegrave, William 160
Wales 4, 5, 6, 71, 122
Welsh nationalists 71, 73
Waterloo, battle 8
Wessex, kingdom 3
Whigs 8
William III (of Orange)
7, 19
William the Conqueror 4
Wilson, Harold 33, 36
Withdrawal Agreement
(WA) 108, 109–15,
121, 124–5, 139
women's suffrage 100
World Trade Organization
(WTO) 100, 138,
139, 142
World War, First 14–15
World War, Second 15, 16,
17–18, 22, 68–9